The Untold Stories from a Correctional Officer

You Can't Make This Sh*t Up

ISBN-13: 978-1-7321186-5-2
ISBN-10: 1-7321186-55
LCCN: 2025900561

First Edition
April 2025

All images outsourced through **Pixabay.com**
unless otherwise noted.
Cover design: J.R. Harris
Fly: https://www.pngegg.com
Editor: William Lovan Jr.

For questions, concerns, comments, please write the author directly at
Heyharris1@yahoo.com

Notable works

Icearaus Flight
Birthright
The Hour of Reckoning

Assisted works

Someone like me

If you want to see the dregs of society, go down to the jail and watch the changing of the guard.

Mark Twain

Hold Harmless Agreement

Hold Harmless: All persons, people, or subjects who read *The untold stories from a correctional officer* shall fully defend, indemnify, and hold harmless James Harris from any and all claims, lawsuits, demands, causes of action, liability, loss, damage, and/or injury of any kind whatsoever (including without limitation all claims for monetary loss, property damage, equitable relief, personal injury and/or wrongful death), whether brought by an individual or other entity, or imposed by a court of law or by administration action of any federal state, or local governmental body or agency, arising out of it, in any way whatsoever, any act, omissions, negligence, or willful misconduct on the part of the author, its officers, owners, personnel, employees, agents, contractors, invitees, or volunteers. This indemnification applies to and includes, without limitation, the payment of all penalties, fines, judgements, awards, decrees, attorney's fees, and related costs or expenses, and any reimbursements to James Harris for all legal fees, expenses, and costs incurred by it.

Enforceability, Severability, and Reformation: If any provisions of this Agreement shall be held to be invalid or unenforceable for any reason, the remaining provisions shall continue to be valid and enforceable. If a court finds that any provisions of this Agreement is invalid or unenforceable, but that by limiting such provisions it would become valid and enforceable, then such provisions shall be deemed to be written, construed, and enforced as so limited. The intent of the Parties is to provide as broad an indemnification as possible under Oregon law. In the event that any aspects of this Agreement is deemed unenforceable, the court is empowered to modify this Agreement to give the broadest possible interpretation permitted under Oregon law.

Agreement: Possession of any and all parts, pages, pictures, articles, of *The untold stories from a correctional officer* by either electronic, digital, print, social media, or any other forms of transfer by way of purchase, gift, found, stolen, acquired, or located on social media constitutes agreement to the **Hold Harmless** agreement.

Introduction

Hello all, and welcome to *The Untold Stories from a Correctional Officer.* What you hold in your hot little hands is unlike any book on the market. Between the covers you won't find a book on how to become a better correctional officer, one single long-drawn-out story about a thirty-year career, nor will you find some governor's speech on how they have the best prison system in the world with the lowest recidivism rate. What you will find are over one hundred of the craziest, most ruthless, bizarre, unexplainable, despicable, and implausible stories to ever grace the pages for the public to view. You see, the correctional complex preaches transparency and accountability in the public eye, yet once the door slams shut and the bolt drops, the prison system is nothing more than a secret society, such as the Illuminati, the Freemasons, or the Knights Templar.

For those who have never set foot inside an institution and have only watched shows like Lock Up or 60 Days In, I regret to inform you that your perception of prison is inaccurate. What you fail to understand is that prisons lead a double life. The first life is the one we would naturally expect. You supervise rapists, child molesters, murderers, drug addicts, arsonists, thieves, and a variety of other criminals without passing judgment, all while maintaining a professional demeanor. The second life thrives in the shadows of darkness, growing stronger in secrecy and hidden from the light of other's scrutiny. Each day that passes unchecked, the second life thrives in this environment of concealment. Mystery and negativity. As we will witness in these pages, the second life, once revealed, will relentlessly strive to retreat into the shadows, where it finds the most comfort, even if it means undermining honesty.

What's even more distressing than the stories in these pages is the realization that management, directors, and governors are aware of this second life, yet they choose to remain silent, allowing it to thrive in the shadows. Without delving into specifics, correctional officers have a suicide rate that is 39% higher, than other law enforcement agencies, PTSD rates that are ten times higher than the general population, a divorce rate that is 20% higher than the national average, and a heart disease rate that is 50% higher than any other occupation. Correctional departments nationwide are striving to advocate for "Officer Wellness" programs, hoping to change public perception while overlooking the underlying issue. Until you hold those responsible for feeding the monster, these numbers will never change for the good.

Regrettably, when staff question the perceived actions of those in management, they often resort to retaliation, humiliation, and gaslighting as weapons. To question them and submit the facts is doing nothing more than signing your own termination papers. They guard the locked doors and control the light switches, keeping what they want hidden in secrecy. After all, why would anyone want to defeat the beast when they themselves are the beast?

Please note that this book was not my idea, but rather the idea of my coworkers, who suggested that I write a book showcasing the craziest things I have witnessed. Please join me as you immerse yourself in stories that range from humorous to deadly serious, instances of management betrayal, staff-on-staff assaults, filthy lies, incompetence, and deceit. I have organized the stories into ten major categories, although many of them overlap. So, without further ado, sit back, relax, and enjoy *The Untold Stories from a Correctional Officer: You Can't Make This Sh*t Up*.

Battle not with monsters, lest ye become a monster, and if you gaze into the abyss, the abyss gazes also into you.

(Friedrich Nietzsche)

izquotes.com

Table of Contents

Table of contents

Table of contents

Miscellaneous stories

Conclusion

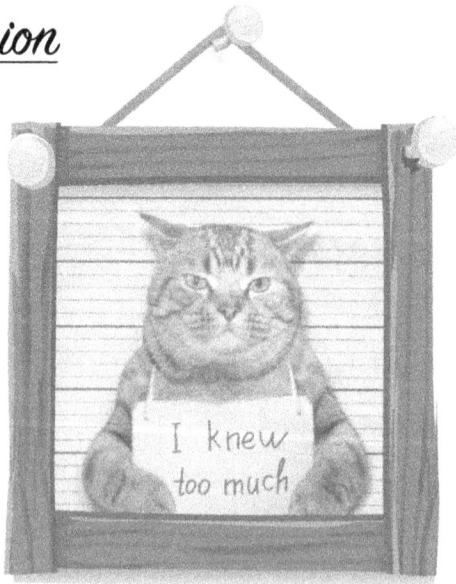

Laughter is the best medicine

Most people are unaware of the numerous protective qualities that laughter possesses. Laughter strongly correlates with happiness and is considered one of the best ways to manage the perceptions of stress and improve psychological sturdiness. Evidence has shown that laughter improves brain function and encourages the growth of new neurons and synapses.

I'm not convinced we've wasted enough time on this.

PSST sickening to a captain's meeting

There is more to laughter than just brain functions, but evidence reveals that laughter also lowers blood pressure, epinephrine, and glucose levels while increasing glucose tolerance. It doesn't stop there, but laughter can also help break the cycle between pain, sleep loss, depression, and immunosuppression.

Many may not understand why this is important, but allow me to explain. Correctional officers face a demanding job that never leaves us. Research reveals that correctional officers experience higher levels of PTSD than combat veterans, have suicide rates twice as high as all other occupations combined, exhibit higher levels of drug use, and have an unprecedentedly high divorce rate. This gets even worse when management is against you, as in this perfect example by a correctional officer who asked a captain, **"How come we don't wear stab vests?"** The captain replied, **"If you get stabbed here, then you probably deserved it."**

We'll leave the light on.

Haynes all the way

Have you ever made a decision you regret? Well, that was me on a warm summer night; I found myself in a situation where I should have called in sick. Had I known what was to occur, I never would have risked the inevitable.

I strolled into roll call, stomach churning and beads of sweat dripping down my face. I should have left at that moment, but instead, I made the foolish decision to stay. With roll call complete, I make my way to my assigned post. After giving a brief briefing, the officer heads to the bathroom to gather his belongings when chaos ensues. The churning in my stomach became unbearable, and I rushed towards the garbage can, initiating a series of vomiting fits worthy of an Olympic gold medal. In the process of filling the garbage with the most vile, disgusting-smelling stuff imaginable, my bowels failed. It felt like the thrust of a rocket as my drawers filled with a warm substance the same consistency as whipped cream. I thought this was the end, but my innards had other ideas and proceeded to fill my drawers with 2 more good, solid squirts. I stood there pale as a ghost, thinking, Well, maybe it's not that bad.

The officer left the bathroom and wished me a good night, oblivious to the events unfolding just ten feet away. As I was considering my next move, my second key, an additional officer who keeps an eye on the unit while you perform the count, arrived. I commence my count by shuffling my feet in a manner reminiscent of a penguin in order to prevent the ungodly matter from causing any further harm than it has already caused. Behind me, the noxious, putrid, rancid odor hung heavy in the stale air. It was a stink that was borderline suffocating and clung to the back of your throat with each involuntary gasp. The smell was so bad, I was shocked that he did not turn and flee with each gasp but instead followed me, sniffing the air with each step. Fortunately, the smell from the unit was already such that he didn't realize it was me and not one of the inmates.

With the officer gone, I stood there, legs closed, contemplating the future. After a minute or two, I had a plan and entered the bathroom. I took off my duty belt, boots, socks, and pants. I stood there, staring at my underwear and the enormous bulge of shit.

Damn, I thought. Whoever made these Haynes deserves a raise, as they held everything perfectly. Not a single stream leaked down my legs. I undressed, stood in the bathroom completely naked, cleaned myself up, and bagged my underwear. But the smell permeated the first bag, so I had to bag them again.

Unpleasant thoughts plagued my mind as I dressed. I am currently free-bagging, and the repercussions of shitting my pants again will be severe. There was no safe barrier between my pants and my ass, which was still grumbling like an irritable volcano.

With no other choice, I called the shift lieutenant and said, "You're not going to believe what happened, but I just shit myself."

He stuttered as he spoke. "You... you... you... you just did what?"

I explained everything in excruciating detail, then waited for a response.

His response was not what I expected. "Do you want to go home?"

I replied, "Yes, unless you can move me somewhere where I have access to a bathroom at all times."

To my surprise, I ended up in segregation where I continued to shit every thirty minutes like clockwork. The moral of the story is, the next time you're sick, remember to call in.

MY MANAGER THE NEXT DAY AFTER I SUBMIT ANONYMOUS STAFF SURVEY

Pen pal

It was the doldrums of the night. The air was stagnant, the tier deathly silent. I stood in the officer's station, staring down the tier, the darkness my only friend. A few cells' windows glowed a kaleidoscope of colors as the TVs inside jumped from one commercial to the next in no particular order. Patiently, I stood there fondling my pen, flicking the pocket clasp to some unknown rhythm embedded deep in my brain.

"God damn it," I groaned as the pen slipped from my fingers and fell with the grace of an Olympic diver towards the floor. Upon impact, the pen did some strange slide only to come to rest beside the recycle bin.

I glanced at my lunch box, trying to remember if I had a spare pen, but quickly realized that this was my last one. I was left with no alternative but to pick up this monstrosity. This thing of evil that tormented me and dared me to pick it up, as if it were possessed.

Placing one hand on the recycle bin, I bent over with the grace of a ballerina. The bin, bearing the brunt of the weight it was never designed to carry, tilted back on the wheels, which screeched like a banshee and began to roll. I had invested too much in my venture to retreat now, and my weight propelled me forward. The bin gained speed and rumbled as if it were on gravel, then shot out like a rocket. With nothing left to grab, I resisted gravity's pull, but gravity won.

Headfirst, I went into the rack that held the toilet paper.

The bin landed partway down the tier leaving a trail of crushed-up cookie boxes and non-aspirin containers as it slid further.

Toilet paper flew as if it had wings as I fought to grab something—anything to keep me from going all the way to the floor. To no avail, I crashed onto the floor, taking the last remaining roll of toilet paper with me.

I gracefully stood up to evaluate the extent of the damage. The cell lights did not illuminate, the phone remained silent, there were no fractured bones, and the pen remained on the floor. Recovering my pen, I then worked in record time to restore the toilet paper rack and recover the bin, picking up the contents as I dragged it back. After cleaning the station, I conducted a more detailed assessment and concluded that my ego was the only casualty.

YOU GOT JOKES

Guy gets to prison, meets his new cell mate, this jacked motherfucker sitting at the edge of the bed.

Cell mate: Listen mate it's going to happen, so let's get this over and done with, would you like to do it with spit or without?

Guy: (Scared) What do you mean?

Cell mate: Would you like to do it with spit or without?

Guy: Well fuck, if I have to I guess I will do it with spit.

Cell Mate: Okay. (Yells) Hey spit he wants you in as well.

OH! The horror

Ungodly secrets lurk in the past, and many skeletons are hidden in closets. However, for some individuals, the adage "Dead men tell no tales" rings false, as they reveal their stories even before they pass away. This incident occurred to an officer who mistakenly believed he had married the love of his life—that is, until one unpleasant night in the bathroom.

His wife, who appeared to be quite large, entered the bathroom and asserted her dominance, interrupting his work. The poor bastard had no choice but to attempt a hasty retreat, only to find himself smashed between an immovable object and her posterior. Time was on his side, though, as her ass looked more like the U.S.S. Truman as it slowly turned. With beads of sweat dripping down his face, he made his way through the gap like a running back heading for the end zone.

Later, we were given the opportunity to hear the story. It appears his wife, who was a tiny woman, was not always like that. In fact, as he told us, she was quite a large woman with a matching attitude. He recounted the terrifying story of that day in the bathroom in great detail. With a distant gaze in his eye, he retold his near-death experience. "She almost put me through the bathroom door," he explained, then continued. "I feared for my life."

The story doesn't end there but grows much more sinister. "She was the worst piece of ass I ever had. "All I ever received from that marriage was a son and a bitch for a wife."

"If we couldn't laugh we would all go insane." – Robert Frost

ON THEIR WAY TO GET MARRIED, A YOUNG CATHOLIC COUPLE WERE INVOLVED IN A FATAL CAR ACCIDENT. THE COUPLE FOUND THEMSELVES SITTING OUTSIDE THE PEARLY GATES WAITING FOR ST. PETER TO PROCESS THEM INTO HEAVEN. WHILE WAITING THEY BEGAN TO WONDER; COULD THEY POSSIBLY GET MARRIED IN HEAVEN? WHEN ST. PETER ARRIVED THEY ASKED HIM IF THEY COULD GET MARRIED IN HEAVEN. ST. PETER SAID, "I DON'T KNOW. THIS IS THE FIRST TIME ANYONE HAS ASKED. LET ME GO FIND OUT; AND HE LEFT. THE COUPLE SAT AND WAITED FOR AN ANSWER.... FOR A COUPLE OF MONTHS. WHILE THEY WAITED, THEY DISCUSSED THE PROS AND CONS. IF THEY WERE ALLOWED TO GET MARRIED IN HEAVEN, SHOULD THEY GET MARRIED, WHAT WITH THE ETERNAL ASPECTS OF IT ALL? WHAT IF IT DOESN'T WORK OUT? ARE WE STUCK IN HEAVEN TOGETHER FOREVER?' ANOTHER MONTH PASSED. ST PETER FINALLY RETURNED, LOOKING SOMEWHAT BEDRAGGLED, "YES," HE INFORMED THE COUPLE. "YOU CAN GET MARRIED IN HEAVEN.." "GREAT," SAID THE COUPLE. "BUT WE WERE WONDERING; WHAT IF THINGS DON'T WORK OUT? COULD WE ALSO GET A DIVORCE IN HEAVEN?" ST. PETER, RED-FACED WITH ANGER, SLAMMED HIS CLIPBOARD ON THE GROUND. "WHAT'S WRONG?" ASKED THE FRIGHTENED COUPLE. "OH, COME ON!!!" ST. PETER SHOUTED. "IT TOOK ME 3 MONTHS TO FIND A PRIEST UP HERE! DO YOU HAVE ANY IDEA HOW LONG IT'LL TAKE TO FIND A LAWYER?"

Nuts

Sometimes, you just never know what you're going to hear. This just so happened to be the case when I was walking out of work. Another officer, who was new and unsure of how to respond to the inmates, was standing beside me. Still, what I heard left me flabbergasted and nearly made me burst into laughter. What you are privy to now is that conversation.

"Harris, you've been here for a while."

"A minute or two," I answered. "Why? What's up?"

He stared off into the distance, not sure how to respond. Confusion laced his words as he spoke. "An inmate said something to me this morning, and I wasn't sure how to respond."

I stopped walking, thinking this might be serious. "What did he say?"

The officer glanced at the ground before turning to face me. "You know they have to have their beds made by 7?"

"Yup," I answered.

"Well, it was a bit after 7, and I told him he needed to get up and make his bed; then he could lay back down. He just grumbled and rolled away from me."

"Was he an early morning worker?" I asked. "They can sleep in later."

"No, he wasn't," the officer said.

"So, what did you do?" I asked.

"I told him he needed to get up and make his bed."

"And?"

He sat up in his bed, looked directly at me, and said, "Who are you to tell me what to do? My nuts have more experience than you."

At first, I chuckled, but soon realized the officer was unsure of how to handle the situation. "Did you tell him to get the fuck up, or you would cell him in?" I asked. "Did you at least talk shit back?"

"I just walked away. I didn't know what else to do. Finally, about half an hour later, he got up and made his bed.

I laughed and said, "If you're going to work here, you gotta learn to give shit back when they give it to you. Given you're new, it is likely that he was simply testing his limits. However, next time just don't play their bullshit games."

Open mouth, insert foot

I might be mistaken, but I believe that everyday people often say things they wish they could take back. Whether it's anger, frustration, irritation, tiredness, a lack of common sense, or sheer stupidity, it happens. Unfortunately, this time it was my time to open my mouth and insert my foot.

The events unfolded while I was en route to the hospital to monitor an inmate. All night, I kept thinking about the paperwork I had submitted a few months ago, eagerly awaiting a response from someone in management, as the deadline was rapidly approaching. Graveyard passed, and it was now dayshift. As I prepared for a long day of overtime, my thoughts still festered like an overripe boil that exploded after about fifteen minutes on the road. All I could see was her face, sitting behind the desk, mocking me as I lost it. I cannot think of one filthy, nasty word that didn't escape my mouth as I vented. I called them a fucking cunt, a worthless bitch who slept her way to the top, wasn't worth shit, and was totally useless. Words cannot express the level of frustration I felt, as I had to invent new terms to describe them.

After about ten minutes of me venting and ranting, saying the most ungodly things and spewing straight drivel, the officer driving the vehicle looked at me with an expressionless face and said, "You know she's my wife?"

For a few minutes, as I gathered my thoughts, I was at a loss for words, so I continued with more venting. "Bullshit, you wouldn't have married a bitch like that." I was so pissed; all I could see was red.

"Really, she's my wife," he continued.

I let a few more minutes pass and then said the only thing I could think of, "Why don't you both have the same last name?"

He looked at me and chuckled, "Because she said it would be easier in the divorce to keep her last name."

At that point, I wasn't sure what to say. The rest of the drive there was relatively quiet, as was the hospital watch. All I could think about was how this would impact my future. Unsurprisingly, a few weeks later, someone called me into the office and asked, "Harris, did you really say this, this, and that?"

It must be getting close to campaign season. We have another politician here for a foot removal.

I briefly believed that the individual had ratted on me; however, upon further reflection, I realized that I had it coming. "Yes, I did," I said, "and a few things you didn't mention."

"Could you please explain why?" they asked.

"I told everything, as I was still pissed why I said what I said."

Soon after the incident, I was delighted to see the paperwork processed on time. I also came to realize that it wasn't the other officer who made the initial statement. I'm aware that a few others have heard about it, but I'm still curious about who relayed my words to management. Oh well, all it makes for now is a funny story.

"**Mistakes** are always forgivable, if one has the courage to admit them."

-Bruce Lee

Compound not clear

Count is the most important aspect of corrections. For the safety of the public, it's imperative that you have all your inmates. All inmates must be in a specific location to ensure a proper count. In the units, they must sit on their bunks. In the kitchen they have to stand against the wall. The institution has implemented a procedure for other areas. The final verification is to make sure the compound is clear.

As we were getting ready for the count, a radio call from control came in, inquiring about specific locations and whether their areas were clear.

"Compound is clear," one officer responded.

My friend, who was working at a different location, received a call asking if his area was clear.

"Control, we have movement on the compound." The call came back.

Since there should be no inmate movement, we all looked out the windows within the units.

"We got movement in the breezeway," my friend continued.

I wondered what the decision-makers were thinking as they searched the cameras.

It was now my buddy who came back on the radio. He said, "Control, there's a cat on the compound."

I almost soiled my drawers laughing.

Control was as frustrated as a mosquito in a mannequin factory.

Later that night when we left, control posted a picture of a cat on the window asking if anyone seen the officers cat? At least they finally got a decent chuckle out of it.

Prison Jokes

Q: Why did the pianist go to prison?

A: He fingered the wrong minor...

A young man goes to jail for the first time.
An older man with numerous tattoos sitting on the bottom bunk asked his new cellmate if he wants to play football.
"Sure," he responds... "but how?"
"Well," the man grins. "You get on the upper bunk and jerk off. If you hit the ceiling with your load, it's a touchdown. Then you have to roll over and fart for the extra point."
"I'm game," the younger man replies.
The older inmate jumps up on the bunk, beats it like it owes him money, then lets out a massive groan as his load hits the ceiling.
"Touchdown," he yells. He flips over and lets out a loud, raspy, nasty fart. "Extra point is good. 7-0, your turn."
The younger, newer guy hops up there and does a marvelous job of splattering the ceiling. "Touchdown," he yells, then flips over.
The older inmate jumps on top of him and immediately begins ramming him in the ass.
"What are you doing?" The younger man screams.
The older man gets down close to his ear and whispers, "Trying to block the kick."

Koi pond

Who would have thought that working in corrections would pay you to go fishing? Well, that's exactly what happened within my first month. Assigned to the mobile, I was uncertain about the process, so I asked for help. The lieutenant assigned another officer to guide me through the process before I proceeded on my own.

We had not been together for fifteen minutes when I experienced an uneasy feeling in my stomach. "What do you do if you have to take a shit?" I ask.

"Just park out front and go in and use the bathroom," he answered.

The bathrooms were located in the admin building, which was about the size of a small gym. In the middle was a large indoor pond a few feet deep that contained a handful of multi-colored koi. I asked my trainer about the koi, to which he explained that the warden owns the pond.

I use the fine facilities and then begin my search for a roll of paper towels. As I rummaged through the cabinets lining the far wall, I discovered an abundance of cans of chicken noodle soup. "That's kind of weird," I mumbled and proceeded with my search. With the paperwork done, I meet the officer who waited by the pond.

"What's up with all the chicken noodle soup?" I ask.

"Oh, you never fished for the koi?"

I could only imagine the look on my face as I answered. "Ah, no," I said.

"Follow me," he chuckles as he walks towards the bathrooms. Grabbing a can, he retrieves an old, dilapidated can opener from a side drawer and proceeds to peel it open.

I patiently watch his every move.

He dumps the can in the sink, carefully selects the chicken, and then feeds the rest to the garbage disposal. From another drawer he snatches a box of inmate dental floss. "Alright, we're ready."

I follow him out to the pond, where he ties a piece of chicken onto the dental floss, feeds out about ten feet of line, then tosses the chicken in the water. After about a minute, the line jerks stiff, and he yells, "Fish on." Working the line with great finesse, he brings this large, multicolored koi to the surface, where it finally gets the chicken free from the knot and then dives back into the depths.

"What the fuck?" I ask.

"It doesn't hurt them," he responds. "It's more like a game."

"Ohhh, can I try?" I ask.

He hands me the bait can and dental floss. "Sure. The only rule is, "If you take a can, replace it."

"Gotcha," I said, as I tied the chicken onto the line and then cast it out.

A minute or two later I yell, "Fish on." I never got my first fish to the surface.

I learned over time that it's an art form that takes months of practice to work the fish just right to get them to the surface.

Magazine cover

There are times when the easiest overtime can also be the most boring. When the opportunity for overtime arose, I chose to observe the stairwell while the elevator underwent maintenance. My buddy was at the bottom, and I was at the top. Our main job was to make sure no inmates fought in the stairwell or passed contraband. When no inmates were there, we would chit-chat about all kinds of miscellaneous things.

It was break time, and another officer arrived sometime after nine. First, she asked my buddy, who was at the bottom of the stairs, if he needed a break, to which he declined. Next, she poked her head into the stairwell and shouted up to me, asking if I needed a break. I said, "Nah, I'm good." Before she left, I yelled back down, requesting permission to ask her a question. She yelled back up, "What?"

I relaxed and collected my composure. "If I were on the cover of a sports magazine wearing nothing but my boots and my duty belt, would you buy it?"

I could only guess what she was thinking, as she nearly vomited at the thought. After a moment, she exclaimed, "That's disgusting."

We were all friends, and we all got a delightful chuckle.

I didn't realize that someone was standing behind me until I heard the words, "I would."

I spun around doing my best ballerina twist only to find a lady who works in medical standing there smiling.

I uttered the only thought I could muster: "Really."

Potty break

Everyone who has a brain slightly larger than a slug knows it's a crime to bring a cell phone into a secure facility. However, some individuals continue to defy the law, confident in their ability to avoid detection. Those who choose to take the risk could face detrimental consequences. In every state, introducing contraband inside a secure facility is considered a Class C felony.

This is the story of a lady who consistently pushed boundaries. I knew she brought her phone in every day, but what did I care? She wasn't letting the inmates use the phone. She believed that the break room did not provide a safe place to leave the phone, and the potential damage from weather changes precluded using her vehicle. The summers were excessively hot, and the winters were excessively cold.

One particular day, her life nearly underwent a dramatic transformation. As we gathered together and engaged in conversation with a lieutenant, a phone rang unexpectedly. You could see the panic in her eyes; you could smell the fear in the air. I remained silent, acting as if I hadn't heard it, but it was clear where the ringing came from.

Without any hesitation, she leaped out of the chair and exclaimed, "That's my alarm signaling that I need to use the restroom."

The lieutenant stood there baffled. I'm unsure if he even knew what to say. Who has an alarm that alerts them when they need to use the restroom?

After she departed for the bathroom, we all remained silent. None of us said a damn thing. We all watched the lieutenant, waiting to see his reaction.

The lieutenant didn't do anything. He hung around for a minute or two, then left.

When the officer returned from the bathroom, she confessed to us all that she forgot to turn her phone off. We all had a delightful chuckle.

No, we are not married

Everyone wants a laugh now and again to lighten the mood, so when the opportunity arose, I took full advantage of it.

My friend, who was on the hospital watch, asked me if I wanted to work overtime. We frequently worked overtime together, so it was not unusual. We got along wonderfully and always had a great laugh.

As we entered the hospital, my friend said she wanted to go get some coffee before we made our way to the room where the inmate was located. We headed to the cafeteria, where the unthinkable began. Upon arrival we begin arguing about coffee. She believes coffee is the next best thing to sex. I disagreed, stating that coffee tastes like a wolf's pussy. We banter back and forth for a few minutes. Eventually, the cafeteria lady intervenes and says, "You two are married, aren't you?"

My friend exclaimed, "Oh, my God," and I was too engrossed in my laughter to respond. Eventually, she gets her coffee, and we leave to take over the hospital watch.

Fast forward to lunch.

I ask her what she wants for lunch. She picks the chicken strips and fries. Okay, all is good. She pulls out her pink credit card and says she is going to pay today, as I paid yesterday. Attempting to argue with her is akin to arguing with a mule. Therefore, I proceed to the cafeteria and place an order for two chicken strip baskets. When the lady mentions the price, I find it incredibly low, so I inquire if she also ordered two.

She responds with, "No, I only got one."

"You better put a second one on there, or my wife will get upset," I said.

It was now the beginning of the end.

The lady says, "I knew you two were married."

I said, "Yeah, she doesn't like to talk about it at work."

The woman then starts talking to me about her fifteen-year marriage and four children.

I tell her we've been married a few years and have one child. Then I tell her that we actually have three kids and that two are from a previous marriage.

She says, "Oh, okay."

I explain how I don't like her other two kids.

With a shocked expression on her face, she spoke. "Well, that's awful mean to say."

I calmly say. "It's not my fault they're Black."

The lady's eyes opened wide as saucers, and her jaw hung loose, not knowing what to say.

After returning to the room and explaining the situation, she blushed intensely and exclaimed, "Oh great." "Now I can never go back in the cafeteria again."

Surprise Story

How did I get the nickname Ragdoll?

Well, my best friend and I were doing overtime at the hospital. The nurse entered and asked if one of us would help her slide the inmate up further onto the bunk as he was slowly sliding down. Well, I got nominated as I was the male.

Before we go any further, you need to know more about the nurse. This lady stood at approximately 6'2, had a weight of 280, and was covered in a thick layer of ink. It wouldn't have surprised me if she said she was conceived on the back of a Harley.

Anyway, I grab ahold of the sheet to slide him up the same time she yanks. I was not expecting her to use such force, and it damn near threw me over the bed, dislocated my shoulder, and all but knocked over all the medical equipment. I damn near stated, okay, I'll go do the dishes; don't hurt me again.

My good buddy damn near shit their pants laughing and stated I looked like a Ragdoll getting thrown around.

I'm sure it did from their perspective, as I was untangling myself from the nest of wires I was dragged into.

For the rest of that day, and I'm not sure how long into the future I was called Ragdoll, but it's all good as I deserved it.

Automatic hole puncher

Guns, firearms, pistols, rifles, hole punchers, bang bangs or whatever you wish to call them, are synonymous with law enforcement. Some law enforcement officers carry them daily, such as the police while those in corrections carry them much less frequently. Regardless of your job, accidents, stupid incidents, or just plain incompetence happens quite often.

The National Safety Council reports that about 1% of all gun deaths, or 535 deaths occur each year from negligent or accidental discharges. That means that more than one person dies from an accident each day.

What's more concerning than the number of deaths, it's the number of law enforcement that are trained to handle firearms that are injured each year by accidental or negligent discharges. In almost every case, the discharge could have been prevented had they followed the simple rules of handling a firearm.

Glock owners

- first time gun owner following the recommendation of a retard, or someone with small hands
- has an RMR, calls people using irons stupid
- has posted 20 chicken drill videos
- falls for hype beast marketing regularly
- thinks it's literally the only acceptable carry option
- will literally die for The Glock brand
- calls it perfection, replaces all the stock parts immediately
- gets mad when you point out the next Gen only changed where the serrations are placed
- the gun equivalent of someone who stands in line for new Apple products

One of my buddies on the PD when I first started was a true gun NUT, he had more guns in his rack then several of the PD's around our area had in total. One evening, he stopped at home for supper, his wife had the television on in the living room, and Gunsmoke was just starting (ya this was a looong time ago). Well for those who have never seen Gunsmoke, it begins with Matt Dillon walking down the street for a gunfight, and when the music is at the crescendo, Matt draws and fires. Well my buddy wanted to outdraw Matt Dillon, he drew and fired as well. He was carrying a .44 Magnum 4 inch Smith and Wesson. Blew the television all to hell, nearly deafened himself and his wife, this almost lead to a divorce, but since we were a small close knit department, he only got an ass chewing from the Chief, and told next time make sure your revolver is unloaded before outdrawing a television.

And here we have another fine example...

"Firearms instructor, other Lakewood cops reprimanded for inadvertently firing their guns"

Last year three officers with the Lakewood Police Department, including a senior officer and firearms instructor, accidentally fired their service weapons when they weren't paying attention, internal investigation records show. One officer was texting when he accidentally fired his gun through the wall of his condo. Another officer was showing off his gun to a coworker when he accidentally fired it through his patrol car windshield. A third accidentally shot a hole through the hood of his patrol car when he exited his vehicle while it was still moving and lost his balance.

Aim elsewhere, please

The night started off like any other: cloudy, with a light breeze, and the same old bullshit in roll call. If I only knew how the shift was going to end, I might not have been so moody as I stumbled towards my unit, one bootlace still dragging behind me, my eyes fixated on the three flights of stairs I was about to climb.

Do count, complete the shower log, put papers away, print a new roster, go through the ID card box to make sure it's accurate, then settle in behind the desk. I was sitting there, with one eye closed, listening to the rhythmic whine of the toilets flushing in the background, when the phone rang. I boot to life and speak into the phone with my most dignified voice. "Officer Harris, how may I help you?" I ask, fully expecting the shift lieutenant to inform me that I'm either stuck or in the bucket.

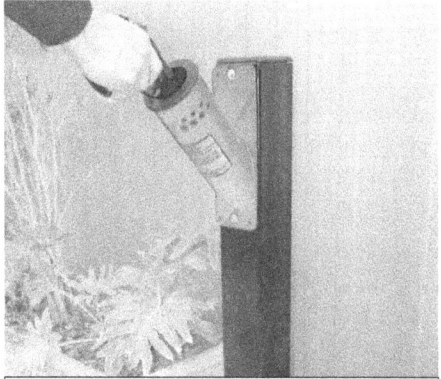

This is a typical pistol clearing station, **NOT** the one actually used in the incident. Its only purpose is to aid the reader in understanding what a clearing station is.

"Check this out, Harris," the faceless voice mumbled.

To my surprise, it's my buddy who drives around the outside of the institution. "How the hell have you been doing, you old bastard?" I excitedly ask as I depart the officer's station and enter the dayroom to prevent the inmates from hearing our conversation.

He chuckles and exclaims, "You're not going to believe what happened tonight."

The tone of his voice assured me that this was going to be a positive experience. "What the hell happened?"

"Well," he says with a laugh. "During the shift change, the officer placed the pistol in the clearing station to clear it, then pulled the trigger, resulting in a bang," he chuckles. I believe he neglected to rack it in order to clear the chamber and remove the mag.

"What the fuck?" I asked, gasping for breath and wiping away the tears. "Did you report the accidental discharge to the lieutenant?" I mumbled while still laughing hysterically.

"It gets worse," he continues, refusing to answer my question. "After the pistol fired, he became agitated, pulled it out of the clearing station, and began swinging it wildly in my direction, cursing and swearing. "I nearly pissed myself as I ducked and dodged the weapon. Eventually, I had no choice but to grab his arm and forcefully point the pistol back into the clearing station."

"You need to report this," I said. "If you don't report this, your ammunition count will be inaccurate."

"Nah," my buddy chuckled. "The officer is going to go home, get a bullet, and bring it back so the count will be accurate in the morning."

"WOW," I said, looking out the window into the darkness.

FIRST LAW OF PHYSICS:

"GRAVITY DOESN'T WORK UNTIL YOU LOOK DOWN"

Lookout below

Gravity works… There is no need to test it. Some people struggle to grasp the concept that dropping something causes it to fall. One officer appeared to have forgotten this concept. We always kept our weapons loaded with a round in the chamber. In case of an incident, you could turn off the safety, aim, and fire. No unnecessary actions.

Two officers posted themselves in the middle of the compound, transforming the roof of a building into a makeshift tower. Barbed wire surrounded the tower, which stood approximately twenty feet above the ground. When a fight broke out near the makeshift tower, this officer proudly racked the shotgun, forgetting he already had a round in the chamber. It's important to note that the initial shot is always a popper round, intended to create a loud noise and indicate your seriousness. The next four rounds are deadly.

Both officers watched as the popper round sailed off the roof and landed on the compound.

If this wasn't disastrous enough, what happened next defies all laws of logical thinking.

The officer who ejected the round leans over to see where it went. He must have had a poor grip on the shotgun because now it tumbled over.

The situation just turned deadly as four officers are busy restraining inmates unaware that a loaded shotgun lies not thirty feet away.

The second officer on the rooftop grabbed his Mini-14 rifle and started screaming at the inmates. "If anyone comes close, I will shoot you dead."

The situation became tense as the inmates stared at the officer holding the Mini-14 and the other officer, who appeared shocked by what had happened. Fortunately, a lieutenant quickly diffused the situation by ordering everyone back to their units, immediately putting the institution on lockdown.

I'm sure it was an accident, but it could have been a deadly one. The institution felt they had no choice but to relieve him of his duties.

!! WARNING !!

Somethings in life you just cannot explain. It is just so god damn bizarre, so erratic, so crazy, you're left with no other choice but to shake your head and say, what the fuck. This just so happen to be the case with something I received, without warning or pre-notice to buy bleach to wash my eyes out with afterward.

Here is a copy of the message I received

I ain't opposed to a little kinkiness alright, but there are certain things I will only do once or never. Peeing on someone is one time thing. Getting a strap on and completely turning someone into a twink little bitch is a never type deal. And yet I've had at least one person ask me to fuck them up the ass with a strap on. Man is still obsessed with me to this day somehow. I ended things when he kept asking for me to violate his ass lmao

Quick draw practice

Some people are just stupid. There's no alternative term to describe them. If you looked up "stupid" in a dictionary, you would find their picture highlighted. This is the story of one of those stupid individuals. Before we can begin, I have to set the scene.

This officer is located in a seventy-five-foot tower, to which only a spiral staircase provides access. At the top, there is a platform, from which a ladder ascends approximately fifteen feet straight up. Now, the design is ideal for preventing tower takeovers. However, this design fails miserably when it comes to rescuing an injured individual.

It was the dead of night and so quiet it hurt my ears. I sat on the tower's catwalk, enjoying the warm night breeze with my feet propped up. The flash and bang of a pistol instantly shattered the silence, to my shock and horror.

I immediately called control and told them what happened.

Control immediately dispatched the mobile to check the tower.

I paced the catwalk the entire time. I just knew this bastard took his own life, and what a shitty place to do it.

A few minutes later a lieutenant arrived at the tower. Up until now, there had been no movement, and the tower and control had no radio traffic. A few minutes later I saw another officer arrive. He must have used the emergency key set to enter the tower. The lieutenant and the officer entered the tower while the mobile officer stayed behind. It seemed like an eternity passed when the scream of a siren broke the silence. The mobile departed to accompany the ambulance to the tower.

I stood on my catwalk watching the whole thing unfold, shaking my head. I couldn't understand why someone would take their own life in such a manner.

It must have been an hour before I noticed the tower officer being brought out on a backboard. The lieutenant secured the scene while the mobile followed the ambulance to the road.

The next day I asked the lieutenant what the hell happened.

He sat back in his chair and thought for a moment. "It seems the officer wanted to improve his pistol drawing skills, given his upcoming visit to the range, and he believed that practicing in the tower would provide an appropriate opportunity." He was alone, so no one could witness him playing with the pistol, and he had eight hours to spare. Apparently, he neglected to unload the weapon for this training scenario, accidentally pulling the trigger and blowing a hole through his foot. To my surprise, the lieutenant thanked me for my actions, stating that my phone call to control likely saved his life. When they arrived, the officer was sitting on the floor, looking pale and shocked.

Despite not facing termination, he never returned to the institution. I guess he didn't want to face the criticism for his stupidity and decided to quit instead.

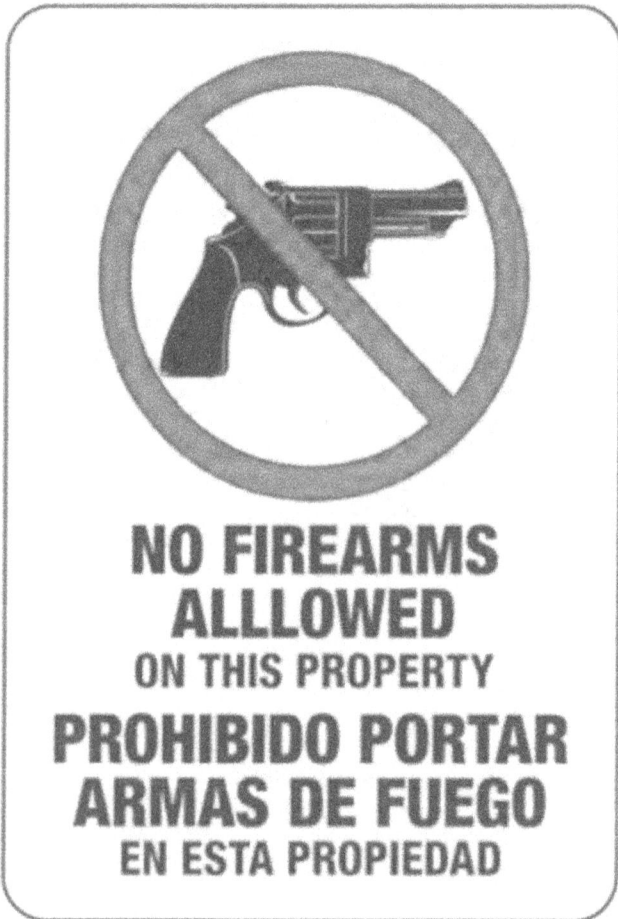

NO FIREARMS ALLLOWED
ON THIS PROPERTY
PROHIBIDO PORTAR ARMAS DE FUEGO
EN ESTA PROPIEDAD

No guns inside

We all make mistakes; that is a fact. However, some mistakes necessitate more severe consequences than a mere reprimand and a vow to never repeat the mistake. This mistake was so serious that it could have resulted in many officers losing their lives on this particular day.

An officer was performing a duty that necessitated the possession of a firearm. No big deal. Working in corrections, we've all had to carry a firearm at least once or twice in our careers.

The problem this time was forgetting the gun and entering the institution.

More concerning than the firearm was the fact that the officer in control, who is at a checkpoint to make sure nothing is brought in illegally, never noticed a big-ass firearm strapped to their side.

Once they passed control, they continued on their way to their next post.

On the way there, not a single person they passed said anything about the firearm. This is quite concerning as we are paid observers. Our training equips us to detect anomalies. Therefore, either people saw the firearm and didn't care, or they weren't as observant as they claim.

They arrived at the inmate dining hall, where they positioned themselves against the wall to oversee the numerous inmates moving around. Eventually, someone alerted her to the presence of a firearm, and she promptly left the institution.

This is a prime example of an uncorrectable mistake. If the inmates had attacked and taken the gun, the situation would have been less than ideal. Fortunately, the removal of the firearm occurred without any incident.

Crawl fucker crawl

The correctional system should not employ a specific group of individuals. They neither have the control to handle verbal conflict nor the common sense to deal with it. Some individuals harbor a power-hungry mindset from being bullied, while others perceive it as a means to elevate their perceived importance. Regardless of their reasoning, some should have chosen a career at McDonald's instead.

This is the story of one individual who took verbal conflict too far.

The officer was working an armed post on a tower in the yard.

An inmate looked up at the officer as he walked past, then yelled, "Fuck you."

The officer responded, "Fuck me; no, fuck you."

The inmate stopped and stared at the officer. My only guess was that he planned to respond to what the officer shouted.

The officer drew down on the inmate with the shotgun, aimed, and then shot him in the face with the popper round.

The inmate collapsed to the ground and then tried to crawl away to safety.

The officer racked the shotgun, putting a birdshot round in the chamber, and shot the inmate in the back.

The lieutenant immediately removed the officer and sent him home pending an investigation. In my opinion, calling the police and immediately arresting him would have been the right course of action. However, a few days later, following the investigation, the police attempted to arrest the officer at his house, only to discover that he had fled back to his home country of Nicaragua. I'm still unsure if he ever faced legal action.

Plane Jane

The day could not have been more beautiful to be at the range. There was a slight breeze, sun, and mid-70s temperatures. This was the kind of day you would have loved to be at the beach, relaxing in a lawn chair, sipping on a frosty drink.

We gathered at the range, put our gear on, and started the day.

The pistol went as expected. Everyone qualified early, and we moved on to the shotgun. This is where the situation got hairy.

I had already finished my turn at the shotgun and was just waiting for everyone else to finish before moving on to the rifle. Leaning against the vehicle not far from us, I observed the unthinkable.

One officer skillfully executed a tactical reload, ensuring his finger stayed on the trigger. As he shoved the shell into the magazine tube, the shotgun moved forward as well. With his finger still on the trigger, the shotgun fired. KABOOOOOOOM.

Oh, that's no good, I thought, then I looked up and my eyes widened. Just as he fired the shotgun, a small plane was passing overhead.

The range master had no choice but to call the institution and let them know what happened.

Fortunately, the plane was too high for the birdshot rounds to ever approach, but I'm sure they would have flinched if they had seen the flash.

We all waited around the range, anticipating a response from the institution. We all had a general idea what they were going to say, but when the call did arrive, it was exactly as expected. We were to shut down, clean up the range, and then report to the institution to write memos on exactly what happened.

Drop the weight

We all detest finding ourselves in a situation where we might have to end someone's life, even if they have earned it. That is exactly the position I found myself in one sunny morning.

I sat at my post, shotgun across my lap, observing the weight pile. As usual, the weights were segregated. The Blacks positioned themselves in the far corner, followed by the Whites in the middle and the Mexicans on the far left. Other smaller groups chose to follow their own path, avoiding involvement in gang activities, but their efforts proved to be futile. Everyone knew that if a big fight broke out, they would either ride with their own race or face death.

Near the exit gate, a scuffle broke out between two white men. It's unclear what exactly happened, but it's likely that the dispute revolved around who had the larger dick or some other trivial issue.

The larger inmate grabbed the smaller man and slammed him to the ground, treating him like a rag doll. He spent the entire duration cursing, swearing, and spitting on the man.

The shotgun was ready to fire, so I raised it high and fired over their heads, yelling for them to get down. Knowing that the first round is always a popper round, the inmates will continue to fight until they hear the shotgun rack sound.

The bigger inmate grabbed a free weight and raised it as if he intended to bash the other inmate in the head.

I yelled for him to immediately drop the weight, or else I would shoot him.

The inmate looked at me. I have no idea what was going through his mind, but he must have thought I was serious as he slowly began to lower the weight.

When the staff arrived on the scene, they restrained both inmates and took them to segregation. That day, a deep sense of relief washed over me, as I loathed the thought of having to handle the paperwork related to his stupid behavior.

Let's all go to prison

> **NOTE:** This story includes names and places as it is all public information as posted in the local paper for all to see, read, and judge.

Hard times and the threat of living on the street can push a man to do just about anything. Most individuals who are unafraid to work manage to find employment, as there are always jobs available. Some individuals experience panic and respond in unconventional ways, resorting to drastic measures that rarely yield positive results. This is the story of one man who chose to lose everything, instead of just some things.

Sergeant Kyker worked at Southern Desert Correctional Facility in Indian Springs, Nevada. I cannot argue one bit that he was a wonderful sergeant, always held the inmates accountable, and taught me more than I could ever imagine. He was a sergeant who always had your back, often referred to as an officer's sergeant. In return for all he taught me, I wish I could have taught him some common sense.

Soon after my resignation and relocation, Officer Kyker's situation took a turn for the worse. His wife was laid off, and they were having trouble paying their bills. (I would have to agree there because Nevada fucks you bad on the paycheck.) Scared to lose everything he had worked for, he did the unthinkable. He and a friend robbed an older woman who was filling an ATM machine. Sergeant Kyker never made it far from the scene. About 5 miles away, authorities arrested him with two cassettes of cash totaling 21,000 and a third cassette containing 84 stamps.

Newspaper Article

Benjamin Kyker is very familiar with the Nevada prisons system, but the veteran prison guard could soon be bunking with the kind of men he's been guarding.

Kyker, a sergeant with the Southern Desert Correctional Center in Indian Springs, was arrested Thursday and faces charges in connection to conspiring with a security guard to rob a bank.

According to his Las Vegas police arrest report, Kyker, 37, went to the Wells Fargo at 10475 S. Decatur Blvd., near Cactus Avenue in the southwest valley, about 10:45 p.m. Wednesday as the ATM was being serviced. placed his .45 caliber Smith & Wesson handgun to the head of the security guard, William Stack, and said, "Give me all you got," the report said. The ATM technician, a woman in her mid-60s, gave the robber two cassettes containing about $21,000 and one cassette of 84 postage stamps. The sergeant then used Stack as a human shield before speeding away in a red Volvo sedan with no license plates, the report said.

But Kyker didn't make it very far. Police stopped his car five miles away, near Rainbow Boulevard and Windmill Lane. Officers say they found the stolen cash and a handgun in Kyker's car.

Kyker told detectives he is an 18-year veteran law enforcement officer who has fallen on hard times. His wife recently lost her job, and the couple couldn't afford to pay their bills, he said.

He also told detectives he was an Army National Guard member, and recognized the bank guard, Stack, as another guardsman.

Automatic hole puncher

"At this point, I felt Kyker and Stack had conspired to commit the robbery," Detective Craig Dunn wrote in the report.

Dunn said he pressed Kyker to tell the truth, and Kyker eventually admitted that Stack had suggested "it would be easy to rob the money for the ATM tech."

Stack told Kyker that "he was guarding an older lady," the report said.

He told police he didn't load his handgun as a precaution against an accidental discharge.

Stack, 25, first told police he didn't know Kyker and hadn't seen the robber's face, but eventually revealed that he knew Kyker for six years through the National Guard.

Stack, who worked with Southern Nevada Security Patrol, said the ATM technician didn't know about the plan and was "very scared" during the robbery, the report said.

Stack and Kyker were booked at the Clark County Jail on charges of robbery with a deadly weapon and conspiracy to commit robbery.

Kyker was being held without bail. Stack's bail status remained unclear; he was not listed in Clark County Jail records Friday.

Kyker told police "he knows what he did was wrong and was very remorseful."

The Nevada Department of Corrections did not return a call seeking comment about Kyker's job status.

Mike Blaskey... Review Journal
Francis McCabe... Review Journal

A businessman was confused about a bill he had received, so he asked his secretary for some mathematical help. "If I were to give you $20,000, minus 14%, how much would you take off?" he asked her.

The secretary replied, "Everything but my earrings."

Special lessons

When you're new to corrections, range day can be terrifying, especially for someone who has never shot before. You're not sure what to expect from the weapon. Is it going to kick hard? Is it going to hurt? What would happen if I made a mistake and failed to qualify? There is a level of tension that is unlike any other aspect of training. Here, a mistake could potentially lead to someone's death.

Some people need more help than others. It's nothing to be embarrassed about or ashamed of. I would prefer to know that you understand what you're doing with the firearm than just be passed because you're a nice person.

The issue arises when there are multiple individuals in need of assistance, but the staff only concentrates on one individual due to her appearance. The next story accurately portrays this situation.

It was range day, and three female staff members were struggling with the pistol qualification process. What should have happened was for the range team to work with each individual, going over everything necessary to help them qualify.

Oh no, that's not what happened. The two range masters dedicated their time to working with the only female they deemed to have a good physical appearance, leaving the other two on their own.

The situation was such that the range masters dedicated their lunch break to working with a single woman, without taking any action to assist the other two. One of the range masters even met with the woman outside of work to dedicate time to improving her shooting skills. The other two women, whom they deemed quite ugly, did not receive the same level of attention.

In the end, all three women qualified, no thanks to the range masters. Such actions leave a negative impression on the employees.

Spinning scope

UGH, range day. Generally, the day is enjoyable and exciting; however, I find the presence of an individual who is constantly observing my every move particularly intimidating. I understand the need for safety, but some people go too far.

We meet at the usual time at the institution and go to the range. We practice with the Glock for the first four hours. As usual, I relentlessly bombard the target with bullets. You could have covered all my shots with a paper plate, with room to spare.

Next, the Mini-14 is where the issues begin. There's no time for practice or preparation; essentially, the range master guides you through the necessary qualifications before you take the test.

To my luck and enjoyment, I get to shoot first. I prefer this because it allows me to get everything out of the way and then relax while watching everyone else. I typically manage to organize everything within a six-inch circle; however, today, I was scattering bullets throughout the entire area. Upon completion, I believe I recorded only four shots out of a total of twenty, and I'm uncertain about the fate of the remaining rounds.

I am acquainted with the range master, and when he observed my target, he exclaimed, "What the fuck, Harris?"

I told him that I think something was wrong with the rifle, as I have never shot that badly, not even when I was drunk.

He assured me that the rifle was fine after zeroing it in that morning.

I called bullshit as he told me I would need to re-qualify.

He handed me back the rifle, and that's when I noticed something wasn't right. The scope was so tight that it would not move when I played with it, but the rifle's recoil caused it to move back and forth and slightly twist in different directions. I demonstrated this to him, and he responded, "Oh, I think there's a problem." I shot with a new rifle and placed everything on target just like I normally did.

A SHORT GUN STORY

A GUY WALKED INTO A CROWDED BAR, WAVING HIS UNHOLSTERED PISTOL AND YELLED, "I HAVE A 45 CALIBER COLT 1911 WITH A SEVEN ROUND MAGAZINE PLUS ONE IN THE CHAMBER AND I WANT TO KNOW WHO'S BEEN SLEEPING WITH MY WIFE."

A VOICE FROM THE BACK OF THE ROOM CALLED OUT,

"YOU NEED MORE AMMO!!!

Never wrong narcissist

Without a doubt, this is the hardest chapter in *THE UNTOLD STORIES FROM A CORRECTIONAL OFFICER* to write. What makes this the hardest is plain and simple, it cuts directly to the bone to demonstrate the mentality of the many who choose the profession of corrections. Every story here comes from past experiences from people I once considered friends, people I would have gave the shirt off my back to help. It was then I was unsure what a narcissist was, until I experienced the full scale of their wraith.

For those people who don't understand what a true narcissist is, I have included the works of Emily Mayfield who offers a no-nonsense approach to how a narcissist functions. I feel this chapter will also be the hardest for readers to swallow as they read (if they read) this. They will no doubt become angry and begin to make excuses, spread lies, or do anything possible to discredit the stories. Be warned though as I've already stated. All the storied between the cover of this book are true.

~If you have a narcissist in your life, you likely have learned they are never to blame, and the fault lies with everyone but them. Narcissists lack accountability in their actions and use blame-shifting to get the focus off themselves. Through the blame-shifting, they never learn how to take accountability, and this maintains the unhealthy way of responding to conflicts and disagreements.

When a narcissist does something wrong, they don't have the ability to accept the wrongdoing. Their inner voice is already so critical so to avoid further injury to their unstable sense of self, they project blame onto others. In people who don't have narcissistic personality traits, they are able to acknowledge a wrongdoing, admit fault, and make changes. To acknowledge fault and accept blame brings a sense of calming and feels good because you have righted a wrong you felt in yourself. To the person with narcissistic personality traits, to accept responsibility doesn't feel good or provide resolution. It brings up more hurt and negative feelings. As a result, the better option for the narcissist is to project blame. The fastest way out of the negative feelings they are experiencing is to put the blame on someone else.

If the narcissist finds themselves in a position where they can't project the blame onto someone else, they feel vulnerable. Vulnerability is an uncomfortable feeling for them that can lead to narcissistic injury, and then narcissistic rage. The narcissistic injury destroys their sense of superiority and grandiosity as their self-esteem and self-worth is being threatened. Their response is rage.

The rage can be through aggressive behaviors, such as yelling, or passive-aggressive behaviors that includes silent treatment or stone-walling. The intended goal is to shut down all communication and restore a sense of internal stability in themselves. They want to turn the focus away from them so that there is no requirement to take blame, even in those situations where escaping blame is difficult.

In addition to narc-issistic rage, the narcissist might also use more pervasive blame-shifting tactics such as gaslighting. Through gaslighting, the narcissist's intended goal is to make you appear to be the crazy one, and to have you believe that you are, in fact, crazy. Gaslighting is a form of control and manipulation where the narcissist designs your reality around what they want you to believe. When the narcissist can gain the upper hand with gaslighting then it leaves their partner always questioning their own reality, which makes it easier for the narcissist to place blame on them when situations come up.

When a narcissist blame-shifts, they don't have to take accountability. However, by not taking accountability for things that are actually their fault, there is no incentive to change. The narcissist will continue to engage in the same unhealthy behaviors, which prolongs this pattern. This is where the projection of blame can not only be damaging to the relationship, but also in the expectation of change in the narcissist.~

~Emily Mayfield/ December 02/2020
~Mindset Therapy

"Narcissists use a calculated (and effective) series of lies and gossip to deliberately bring their target down and make themselves look good. There can be many reasons such as you seeing them for who they really are, to discredit you should you decide to expose them, jealously, resentment, feeling threatened by you, or a simple disagreement. The victim of a smear campaign often finds themselves isolated and or ostracized by family and people who they once thought of as friends."

~Jenni Kerswell-Frost
~Psychotherapist

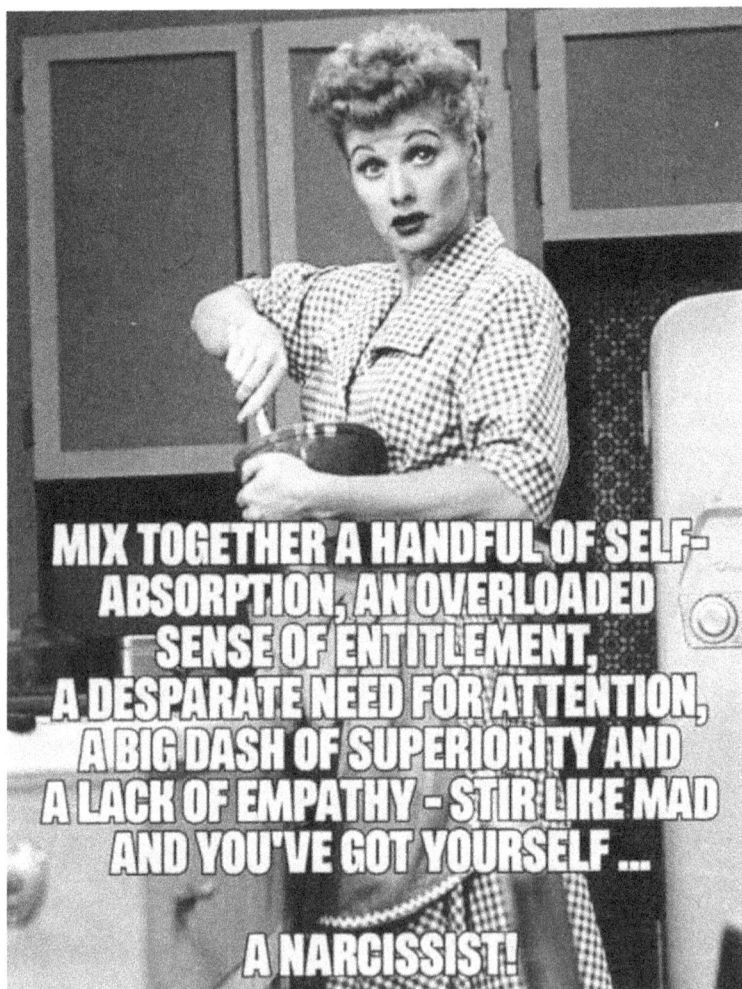

MIX TOGETHER A HANDFUL OF SELF-ABSORPTION, AN OVERLOADED SENSE OF ENTITLEMENT, A DESPARATE NEED FOR ATTENTION, A BIG DASH OF SUPERIORITY AND A LACK OF EMPATHY - STIR LIKE MAD AND YOU'VE GOT YOURSELF ...

A NARCISSIST!

Tracing my steps

Many words could describe my life in the past. Poverty would be an apt term to characterize my life, as I grew up impoverished, living in a barn in southern California and relying on my meager resources. From there, I relocated to a closet in a studio apartment, where each floor shared a single bathroom. I channeled my creativity into crafting dungeons from the D&D books I found in the apartment dumpster, despite having few friends and living alone in the hallway. Even when I joined the military and fought through Desert Storm, my future was always unpredictable. I could have been any one of the soldiers who never made it home. The one word, though, that I feel describes me the best is loyal. To those few people I let into my secluded life, I will defend with a vigor unlike the world has ever witnessed.

My unwavering loyalty is both a burden and a blessing. When I meet someone who I believe is a friend, I return that friendship with honor. What I have discovered all too often is that those who I feel are friends do not reciprocate the same feeling. Once I meet their needs, they move on. Not very often, but on occasion, you meet someone who you feel is a true friend. You would willingly lend a hand or complete their shift to relieve their fatigue. You do not object to performing these tasks, despite the fact that they are taxing on your body, as it is a customary act of kindness among friends.

We expected a true friend to be present, but instead, they displayed their genuine narcissistic behavior. We had an event planned and a date and time picked. My friend informed me that they couldn't attend the event at that time due to scheduling conflicts. I went out of my way to get the time changed, even paying a bit extra, but never complained or asked for the difference.

When I arrived at work that night, they asked me if I wanted to work in the yard or the hospital for overtime. I went to the hospital so my friend and I could get off together. That morning I texted them and told them I would be working at the hospital with them. They asked me what time I would be getting off. I responded with the usual time. They informed me that they had received approval for their time-off request and would be departing early. I questioned why they hadn't notified me earlier, as this would have allowed me to work in the yard and leave at the same time.

Now, their genuine narcissistic nature became apparent. They began yelling and screaming at me, demanding to know why I was tracking them. Why are you looking at my schedule? I don't have to report to anyone but my husband and kids."

I responded with I am not tracking you or looking at your schedule. Notifying me about changes is a common practice among friends, and I firmly believed that we were friends.

> True friends are those rare people who come to find you in dark places and lead you back to the light.
>
> Steven Aitchison

It was now that she rambled about how she is not responsible for not telling me about getting the leave approved and that what she does is none of my business.

Again, I reiterated that it would have been nice if she had informed me of the change.

They displayed a new level of narcissistic behavior when they claimed they were too tired to discuss the issue, a common tactic used by narcissists who have no justification for their actions. fortunately, the friendship has deteriorated due to the narcissist's reluctance to acknowledge their mistakes or apologize, as it could damage their fragile ego.

THE JOKE IS ON THE NARCISSIST ONCE YOU RECOGNISE THIS

What time is it

How many times do you fail to see something until you step back and take a better look? In this particular incident, I mistakenly believed that my friend was having a delightful time joking around. Now I realize it was his narcissistic nature. Unfortunately, I allowed it to unfold, oblivious to the reality that my friend is a narcissist who is determined to destroy everything and everyone who stands in his way.

While working in the yard, I mistakenly called the sergeant on the radio to inform him that the yard was ready for entry. Almost immediately, my buddy got on the radio announcing to the sergeant, "Don't worry, sergeant, I'll call my yard in at the right time."

Another narcissist came on the radio and said, "Yeah, we'll bring our yard in at the appropriate time."

I remained silent, understanding that I had made a mistake and would take responsibility for it. Once I left the yard, I apologized to the sergeant. He said not to worry about it. It was only ten minutes.

My two friends never showed up to share a delightful laugh. They exploited the incident to discredit me in front of the entire institution, bringing it up at every opportunity. Most people would have let it go after a laugh. Not these two. Their aim was to enhance their reputation within the institution, whereas I was perceived as a failure.

Lesson learned. It's crucial to maintain a close relationship with your enemies and a closer relationship with your friends, as you never know when a friend may be deceitful.

Don't talk to me about loyalty. I'm still holding the secrets for the people who are throwing dirt on my name.

Story Break

They know the damage they caused. They know how they twisted the knife.

How they used your kindness, your trust, and your love against you. And now when all their lies and manipulation start unraveling, they panic because deep down they're terrified that people will see them for who they really are.

So, what do they do? They go on the offensive trying to make you look like the villain. Suddenly, you're the one who didn't try hard enough. You're the one who wasn't understanding, or here is the best one. You're the one who abandoned them.

Isn't it rich how quickly they rewrite history to paint themselves as the hero or the victim.

When they were the ones holding the matches, lighting the fires that burned everything down. And they do it so convincingly, don't they? That's the part that really gets to you.

They spun their web of lies so intricately, so perfectly, that even some of the people around you start to believe it. They start questioning you, doubting your side of the story. Wondering if maybe you did something wrong.

That's how good they are at playing the victim. They rewrite the script and everyone plays along, but not you.

You didn't do shit

Most narcissists are self-centered, vile, and loathsome creatures who are more concerned with their own perception and how others view them. They often prioritize their image over the needs or feelings of others, even if their actions could potentially lead to their death. This is one such story.

Several staff members responded to an incident on a unit. Once they arrived on the unit, they made the collective decision to wait until medical arrived. Meanwhile, another officer left the break room after hearing that there was blood involved.

Medical arrived at the unit.

The newly arrived officer saw that the other officers were watching the inmate but doing nothing.

Medical personnel bypassed the waiting staff and went directly to the inmate.

The officer approached the inmate, took him down, and cuffed him.

Staff then escorted the inmate to medical.

Enter narcissism... Shortly after the incident, an officer started claiming that her husband was the one responsible for cuffing the inmate, implying that if he hadn't been present, the outcome could have been unpredictable. For many days she spread the rumors that it was her husband who did it all, when in fact he did nothing but stand there and watch.

A few weeks later we met to discuss the events of that day.

One officer explained that they waited because they were not sure if the inmate had a weapon. An unfortunate aspect of this situation is that they allowed the medical personnel to pass through. You never allow the medical personnel to proceed until you have secured the situation.

When I pointed this out to the officer during the meeting, he became agitated and left. His wife remained there, trying to make excuses for her husband and the situation.

We could have learned something that day to improve the situation next time, but their narcissism and refusal to admit guilt prevented us from doing so. We learned absolutely nothing from this situation.

"PRIORITIZE STAYING IN FAVOR WITH AUTHORITY FIGURES..."

Stealth narcissist

Sometimes the narcissist is the last person you expected. This incident occurred when I sought assistance from the lieutenant. I conveyed to him the circumstances, the accusations against me, and my commitment to fulfilling my duties.

The lieutenant listened to me intently, taking in every word. When I finished, he 100% agreed with me. He said, "You did exactly what I expect from my officers. I expect you to go to the assigned area, offer them a break, and then sign the logbook. You did nothing wrong and have nothing to worry about."

After our discussion, I relayed to him my argument with the captain — *the captain informed me that I misunderstood the situation and that she had called to say she didn't need a break, so I had no need to go over there. I attempted to clarify the situation to the captain, but he failed to grasp the nature of my role. I explained that my job is to go there and offer a break —* and then asked him to explain the situation to the captain.

Upon revealing the captain's response to the lieutenant, he swiftly retreated, asserting, "I can't step on the captain's toes. I hope you understand, he signs my paycheck."

This was not the response I expected. I expected the lieutenant to do the right thing, even if it meant offending superiors.

Then it dawned on me like a divine gift, as if the hand of God reached down and enlightened me. A narcissist's primary focus is on maintaining a positive image and preserving their power within the hierarchy, which means they prioritize staying in favor with authority figures to avoid any potential threat to their status or position.

Yes, the one employee I really thought I could go to in my time of need revealed his true colors.

How do narcissists save money on their electricity bills?

They use gaslighting.

Pencil whipper

Many checks are necessary in the correctional field to ensure inmate safety, institution security, and public safety. These checks may include ensuring that doors remain locked, securing cells, and correctly completing counts, among other things.

One specific post inspects the fences for any damage and ensures the microwave system is functioning properly in case an inmate attempts to climb over them. Other checks include verifying the locks on the doors and the security of the windows on the outbuildings.

The officer begins by checking the fence on one side of the institution. Stationed outside the fence, an officer in a vehicle confirms with control that the microwave is operational. Once the confirmation is complete, the officer proceeds to the opposite side of the institution to conduct a similar check on the other fence. Once the checks are complete, the officer informs control.

Narcissist do not tolerate being criticized, being wrong, being held accountable, or being presented with evidence of their wrong doings.

Anyone who tries to stand up to a narcissist not only has to face the narcissist, but also has to face all of the flying monkeys.

For an undisclosed reason, the shift sergeant concluded that the officer was not conducting his routine checks. Even now, I continue to be perplexed as to how he came to that conclusion, given the existence of cameras throughout the route and the presence of an officer in the vehicle to verify the checks and control, who then turns off the alarm and documents the microwave's operation.

It all began innocently enough with a simple statement about how quickly the officer did his checks, as the lieutenant could not do them that fast.

The officer responded by asking the sergeant to come along and verify he was doing it right. This is a big no-no in the world of a narcissist, as it's a proven fact that they (the narcissist) hate being proven wrong.

A couple of weeks passed, and the officer believed everything was fine; that was, until the shift lieutenant at roll call confronted the officer about not doing the fence checks properly.

To say the least, the officer was flabbergasted by what he heard. How is this even conceivable, and why are we engaging in this discussion? The officer explained that he and the sergeant already discussed the fence checks and that he offered to have the sergeant come with him to verify he was doing it right, but the sergeant refused. The lieutenant said that he would go, but to my understanding he never did.

Once again, this is nonsensical, as the lieutenant could easily sit in control and observe for himself how the officer performed the fence checks. To a normal person, this makes no sense, but to a narcissist, it makes perfect sense. You see, a narcissist can never be wrong. To even suggest that a narcissist is wrong will bring out a fury the world has never seen before. This is precisely what transpired: rather than expressing his error, the sergeant unleashed a vicious attack on the officer.

Don't argue with a narcissist. Their lies are their truths, and they want to watch you going crazy trying to prove it.

Baseball pro

For most people, being a correctional officer was not their first job. Some people worked in construction, other people worked in manufacturing, and even a few may have dabbled in the retail sector. It is rare to come across an individual who played a professional sport before turning to corrections. I know it's difficult to believe, but that's exactly what this sergeant claimed.

The evening started out simple, with minor chit-chat—nothing major. Soon it turned to past experiences, and the sergeant began bragging about how he played professional baseball before starting corrections.

This guy could not possibly have played professional baseball. I doubt it was even possible for this fat little chubby bastard to play on the local softball team.

I confronted him, asserting that he had no professional baseball experience. Well, he began to argue, stating that he indeed played.

I asked him what years he played and for what team.

He responded without hesitation, making it sound plausible. There was no guessing or delay. Being the sleuth that I am, I researched the team and the years, and to my surprise, he wasn't included.

When I confronted him with this newfound information, he responded with yet another round of excuses. His excuses ranged from a printing error to his current absence due to an injury. The blatant lies he was telling shocked me.

Then it hit me. These were not lies to him; they were the truth. Remember, a narcissist never lies.

I decided the best option then was to walk away; it was not worth arguing, as you can never win.

Help me not

Coworkers in the corrections industry develop a certain camaraderie. After all, we work in an extremely dangerous field. Every day, assaults and even fatalities occur against correctional officers across the nation. Therefore it makes sense that we would all help each other out.

A narcissist does not look at the job of corrections the same way as a normal person. To them, everything revolves around themselves. We can observe the same treatment in this particular situation.

The job requires one person to conduct checks on one side of the institution, while another officer conducts checks on the other side. When one officer finishes his checks, he meets the other and gives them the keys to check the other side.

> **The only thing a narcissist changes is how to manipulate better. Get away from these demons.**

The narcissist sees this procedure differently. They hold the belief that they don't need to be in the designated location. The other officer is not responsible for finding and giving them the keys. When called out on their behavior, they make excuses, putting the blame back on the other officer.

This was not an isolated incident but occurred nearly every night. Whenever the officer attempted to transfer the keys to the other officer, the narcissist never appeared in the expected location. He called the narcissist out on the radio and then faced ridicule, harassment, and mistreatment simply for carrying out his duties. At one point, they were summoned to a meeting, but it yielded no results, as a narcissist is adept at portraying themselves as the victim, while manipulating the situation.

Q: How many narcissist does it take to screw in a light bulb?

A: 1, they hold the bulb while the world revolves around them

Show me the money

Narcissists are vile, loathsome, disgusting creatures intent on destruction. What exacerbates their behavior is when they employ their tactics to harm an innocent individual solely for their personal financial benefit. It's a commonly known fact that narcissism, money, and greed go hand in hand. They love spending money, especially when it is someone else's. When the opportunity arises, they can't stand back and refrain from intervening for personal gain.

The situation started when a relationship between two officers deteriorated. These officers engaged in a consensual sexual relationship without marriage. One officer had a second relationship, which is the issue. Feeling guilty about the consensual sex, the narcissist saw an opportunity to strike and intervened. The narcissist concocted a scenario in which he claimed that the officer had sexually assaulted her and that he would serve as a witness. Well, this set off a change of events that would alter the lives of so many people; it was disgusting.

The officer was arrested and charged with a crime, fired from his employment, and financially destroyed—not to mention the horrible reputation that followed from supposedly committing such a heinous crime.

The narcissist was bragging about how she was going to win millions in a lawsuit. Not only did he tell this to me, but he also shared it with numerous other staff members.

As the case proceeded, the narcissist one day came to my unit to offer me a break. As I was getting ready to leave, he told me that all he wanted out of this incident was enough money to pay off his house and truck.

I ignored his words, dismissing them as mere nonsense. Looking back now, I can see his devious intentions for what they really are. He was willing to ruin another officer's life for his own financial gain.

Eventually, the accused officer was cleared of all charges due to his innocence, and karma struck the narcissist, as he received nothing in return. Nothing except for a negative reputation.

A NARCISSISTS INNER IMAGE

MOST NARCISSIST ARE OBSESSED WITH MONEY. THEY THINK ABOUT HOW MUCH MONEY THEY HAVE, HOW TO GET MORE OF IT, HOW TO KEEP IT AWAY FROM OTHERS, AND WHO TO MANIPULATE TO GET MORE OF IT.
MONEY IS THEIR SUBSTITUTION FOR LOVE, WARMTH, AND AFFECTION. HAVING AS MUCH MONEY AS POSSIBLE, EVEN STEALING IT AWAY FROM FAMILY MEMBERS IS THE UNWAVERING GOAL THOUGHTS OF OBTAINING MORE MONEY ARE ALWAYS ON THE NARCISSIST MIND. HAVING AN ABUNDANCE OF MONEY MAKES THEM FEEL MORE ENTITLED AND SUPERIOR TO OTHERS.
~ALEXANDER BURGMEESTER

Post abandonment

Some individuals simply don't care about anyone else. In their eyes, it's all about them. This is a type of narcissist known as grandiose, exhibiting a sense of entitlement, lack of concern for others, and a tendency to exploit those around them for personal gain. Other traits of a grandiose narcissist are an inflated sense of self-importance, a need for admiration, and a lack of empathy for others.

We can see the grandiose narcissist come to life in this next story. The officer agreed to work four hours of overtime. We greatly appreciate anyone who chooses to work overtime. The problem arises after their four-hour shift ended, and the officer departed the institution, effectively abandoning their post without notifying the shift lieutenant. That is a pure violation of the rules, policies, and procedures. Regardless of how long you agreed to work, overtime or not, you cannot leave your post until you receive proper relief.

What the officer should have done was call the shift lieutenant and notify them that their relief has not arrived yet. This way the lieutenant could get an extra staff member to relieve them properly. By keeping their departure a secret, they placed the remaining staff in a precarious situation where things could have escalated. If an assault occurred and the remaining staff called for help, this would be problematic.

It was not until about forty-five minutes had passed that the remaining officer realized that the officer on overtime had departed the institution. When the remaining staff member called the lieutenant, the lieutenant responded, "That officer _____ should be there." Well, officer _____ was not there yet and had not even come through control yet.

The lieutenant sent another staff member to help if needed. Abandoning your post can lead to severe consequences, but as most managers are narcissistic themselves, I doubt anything will come of their actions.

Do the paperwork

Why do some people treat others poorly and believe they are superior to everyone else? I'll tell you why. They are filthy, vile, nasty narcissists who have no purpose in this world except to cause harm, hate, and discontent.

This narrative tells the story of an officer, hereinafter known as the narcissist, who took a new staff member with them when they went to give a break to a unit officer. Upon arriving on the unit, the narcissist decided that instead of giving the officer a break, he would take the new officer (who just happened to be female) and do a cell search instead.

> ## You will never get the truth out of a narcissist.
>
> The closest you will ever come is a story that either makes them the victim or the hero, but never the villain.

The unit officer was expecting his break, so he walked down to the cell where they were located and looked inside. The two officers were sitting very close to each other on the bunk, and the new staff member gave the unit officer a look that said, "Please get this creep away from me."

After the narcissist finished the search, he and his tagalong walked to the officer's station, where he instructed the unit officer to write up the paperwork for the search.

This is exactly what I would expect from a narcissist, as they seem to have a sense of entitlement. Because of their belief that they are perfect and superior, they expect special treatment and wish for people to admire them. They may perceive failure to comply as an attack on their authority and superiority. A narcissist often perceives a person who disobeys their authority as difficult or awkward, leading them to denigrate them or their opinions, particularly in public.

Given this knowledge about the narcissist, it came as no surprise when the unit officer told him NO! You did the search; you do the paperwork. The narcissist saw this refusal to comply with his request as a blatant attack. What made matters worse was the presence of a witness. This infuriated the narcissist to such an extent that he refused to offer the unit officer a break and instead stormed off the unit. After some time, the narcissist instructed his wife to return to the unit and complete the necessary paperwork. To face the man who shut him down in front of another staff member was more than he could bear.

Inside a narcissist mind

LET'S TALK ABOUT A STORY WE ALL KNOW TO WELL. THE STORY OF BETRAYAL OF BEING WRONGED AND YET SOMEHOW, THEY, THE ONES WHO HURT YOU HAVE THE AUDACITY TO PLAY THE VICTIM. ISN'T IT FUNNY, TWISTED REALLY. THEY STAB YOU IN THE BACK, THEN CRY OUT IN PAIN AS THOUGH IT WERE YOU WHO WHO PLUNGED THE KNIFE. THE REAL IRONY IS THEY TRY TO FLIP THE SCRIPT, REWRITE THE NARRATIVE AND SUDDENLY THEY'RE THE ONES SUFFERING. THEY'RE THE ONES WHO WANT SYMPATHY, WHEN ALL ALONG IT WAS YOU WHO WAS LEFT BLEEDING. HOW DOES THAT EVEN WORK? YOU KNOW THE TYPE, THE MANIPULATORS, THE DECEIVERS, THE ONES WHO CAN'T FACE THEIR OWN REFLECTION BECAUSE DEEP DOWN, THEY KNOWN WHAT THEY'VE DONE. THEY CAN'T STAND THE TRUTH. SO WHAT DO THEY DO? THEY PLAY THE ROLL OF THE VICTIM. THEY START ACTING AS THOUGH THE WEIGHT OF THE WORLD IS ON THEIR SHOULDERS, AS IF THEY'VE BEEN MISTREATED, ABANDONED, LEFT OUT IN THE COLD. BUT YOU, YOU KNOW THE TRUTH AND NO AMOUNT OF CROCODILE TEARS CAN WASH AWAY THE TRUTH. THEY ACT LIKE THE WORLD OWES THEM SOMETHING, IN REALITY, THEY OWE YOU EVERYTHING.

Incompetent, inept, or unqualified. You decide

I don't understand why, nor can I explain the phenomenon known as promotional ineptitude. To be fair, you will never find this term in any psychological book, surgical guide, or medical pamphlet. If you search the history of all known psychological ailments, it will evade your every search. The reason for this is that the word doesn't exist. It's a combination of two simple words to bring into reality what I witness every day.

To understand the meaning, we must break down the term into its simplest form. The first word, promotional (n), means the advancement of someone to a more important rank or position. The second word, ineptitude (n), means a lack of skill, ability, or competence. When you combine the words promotional ineptitude, the prognosis is rather simple.

> **Promotional ineptitude (n):** As an individual
> within the ranks of a company or setting moves to
> a more important position, they become
> incompetent, lack relative skill of the job, and lose
> the ability to complete their job in an effective
> manner.

Not all skills are lost though; some are enhanced, adjusted, improved, or perfected. These skills involve the extremely rare but quite effective art of blowing smoke up your ass. Keeping a face chiseled in stone as they lie through their teeth while keeping a forked tongue hidden. The all-effective ability to feed you apple pie-flavored bullshit so you don't choke, and lastly, the ability to vanish the entire shift.

The stories in this section all relate to incidents that will leave you wondering how they made it through life this far with catching their tongue in a blender or the junk in a fan. The things you read are so ludicrous, so bizarre, so unbelievable you'll see corrections in a completely different light.

THE HARDEST PART OF MY JOB IS BEING NICE TO STUPID PEOPLE

Med trip

Although I could have also classified this incident as narcissistic, I decided to include it in this category to give the supervisor a chance.

I was working the compound, observing the inmates as they walked to and from chow, when the radio broadcasted a man-down call. I, along with another officer on the compound, promptly responded to the call. Upon my arrival, I quickly assessed the situation and determined that the inmate would require a wheelchair escort to medical facilities.

The medical team arrived shortly after I made the call, conducted their own assessment, and decided that the inmate should go to the infirmary.

I and the other officer escort the inmate to the infirmary and then return to the compound. I knew we were short-staffed, but I fully expected management to step out of their office and help. I discovered later that no staff had been monitoring the compound during the escort. I thought, "How is that even possible?"

Once chow was over, I entered the lieutenant's office, where two captains were just yapping away and drinking coffee. I clarified that it would have been beneficial if they had monitored the compound during the man-down and escort procedure.

One of the captains looked at me, completely baffled, and asked me why. "We were monitoring the radio traffic during the man-down and didn't hear anything unusual."

"We have three med trips out and are short-staffed," I informed the captain, pointing out that no one was monitoring the compound.

The captain looked directly at me and said, "I didn't know that." He looked at the other captain and asked, "Did you know there were three med trips out?"

The other captain responded that yes, he did.

The captain became agitated and blamed the sergeant for failing to inform them that they needed to monitor the compound.

Excellent way to shift blame. The real issue at hand is that neither of the captains was willing to put down their coffee cups, step up, and offer assistance. They could not accept blame for their own wrongdoings, and it's much easier to shift the blame onto someone else.

Later that day, I had a conversation with the sergeant, who informed me that he had received a stern reprimand for not having anyone on the compound or for not calling to request help.

Once again, an excellent way to tarnish the image of another staff member is to protect your own self-image.

Which hospital

I would think a prison would always know where its inmates are. Perhaps this isn't always the case within the institution, given that inmates often have a variety of responsibilities, such as callouts, work, counseling, medical visits, and other obligations. What I mean is that they should be aware of their whereabouts, especially when traveling outside the institution.

When I arrived at the institution, they informed me that they would place me under hospital watch. Fantastic, easy money. Control notifies me of the inmate's hospital location as soon as I receive the keys.

My friend and I head off to the hospital. Upon our arrival we check in at the front desk, and the receptionist tells us that there are no inmates currently at the hospital.

When I call control, they confirm that the inmate is at that hospital and provide us with the room number.

Great. We now have some information to work with.

We let the receptionist know which room the inmate should be in.

She glances at her computer and shakes her head. That room is empty, she tells us.

After exhausting all our options, we resort to the only remaining course of action. We waited until the door to the back opened, then we slipped inside. Believing we were safe, we inadvertently collided with the receptionist, who was vehemently expressing her dissatisfaction over our difficult return, before she swiftly led us back to the waiting room.

After debating the situation, my friend came up with a brilliant idea. He called control and asked them for the number to the other cell phone.

Control asked why.

My buddy tells control that we still cannot find the other officers. Control reassures us that the inmate is there and in that room.

My friend calls the phone that the current hospital watch has, and lo and behold, they are in a different hospital. Having received this information, we depart for the other hospital. After relieving the other staff, we call control and let them know where the inmate is at.

This is where it really turns stupid. After our shift, we are eagerly awaiting the arrival of our relief. The minutes stretch into hours, yet nothing happens. I contacted control, and they assured me that our relief was on the way.

With no other option, we waited. What else can we do? We can't leave the inmate there alone. To our luck, my buddy just happened to be close friends with our relief officers, so they had his number and called him.

After an explanation, they were on their way.

Upon their arrival, they apologized for being so late and informed us that control had informed them the inmate was in a different hospital. I laughed and told them that control had sent us to the wrong hospital as well. I proceeded to inform them that I had notified control about the inmate's actual location to prevent our relief team from making the same mistake. I guess control doesn't know how to document a damn thing.

Count time

The inmate count is the most important thing you do in corrections. You must check that all inmates are present and in the right place.

During count time, there is to be no inmate movement unless authorized by the HMFIC (Head Mother Fucker in Charge). Therefore, when control announced the start of count time, none of us anticipated what would happen next.

I was sitting in the inmate dining room waiting for the count to clear, positioned at a table where I could look out the large window onto the compound. To my surprise, I observed two inmates walking towards the dining hall. I turned to my friend, who had his back to the window, and asked if the count cleared. He replied with a stern no. We still have twenty minutes, he continued.

"Then why the hell are two inmates walking in this direction?" I asked.

"No, there's not," he said as he turned around, then spit out, "What the fuck."

The two inmates proceeded towards us, walking past a few staff members who remained silent.

After exiting the dining hall, we stopped the inmates and asked them what the hell they were doing.

Only one inmate spoke, stating that the officer had released them and instructed them to immediately go to the dining hall.

"Really?" I said.

The inmate continued his story, saying they even informed the officer that they weren't supposed to be out, but the officer threatened to discipline them if they didn't leave.

I informed them that they needed to return to their unit, and I would contact the officer on duty.

When I seen the officer, I asked them why they sent the two inmates to the dining hall.

The officer stated that they received instructions to send the inmates after the count was complete. I kindly explained that what the dining room officer meant was to send them after the count cleared.

After that, I had a conversation with the dining room officer, ensuring they understood that sometimes we are interacting with new staff members who might not understand and interpret things literally. Next time, please ensure that they are sent after the count clears, not after you have finished counting. This time we got lucky, as there was no harm nor foul, but it could have been disastrous.

Bonus story

I was working my unit, and it was time for the 2:30 a.m. count. As usual, I complete my count and verify it with my roster. Kick back, relax, and wait for the count to clear. To my surprise I get a call from control telling me I have a recount.

WTF, are you sure? Yup, they say. Okay, so I do count again. This time, the count is completed about 15 minutes later, at which point the control officer calls and requests a memo. When I inquired about my mistakes, the control officer informed me that I had marked the wrong bunk. I demand to see my previous count sheet, but they are unwilling to provide it.

Fine, they don't want to show me my old count sheet; fuck 'em.. I write my memo and say, "I fucked up; I'm human; it will probably happen again.

That night when I come into work, the shift lieutenant pulls me aside and says, "Um, Harris. I'm going to need a new memo from you and a memo on the proper way of doing a count."

I just laughed about it, and to this day I have still never written either of those memos. If they don't reveal my mistakes, I won't be able to write a proper memo.

How many doors open

Some people are just so goddamn stupid that you wonder how the hell they found their way out of the uterus. One captain should have been immediately fired, walked out, slapped, and then instructed not to return, not even to bring back his uniforms.

The institution believed it was a fantastic idea to host a huge family event, completely aware that we are seriously short-staffed. To justify the event, the captain had non-security staff work it. Once again, it seems like a fantastic idea, but many non-security staff lack the security mindset to perform the job properly.

I must say the family event was a huge success for both the inmates and the families. Children got to see their fathers while playing games in the yard. Wives got to visit with their husbands, and they all enjoyed a decent meal.

Upon completion, the situation deteriorated. The captain underestimated the time required to remove all visitors and search all inmates for contraband before the count. To counter the time deficiency, the captain made the rash decision to open all the doors leading out of the institution, allowing the visitors to walk out unhindered.

It's important to remember that this is a correctional facility with rules, policies, and procedures in place to prevent an inmate from escaping. I'm sure somewhere in those rules, policies, and procedures, it's highly frowned upon to have all the doors open at once, especially through control, where one door is not allowed to be opened until the other door is closed.

Coupled with the fact that every door was open, it was the job of non-security to supervise the visitors leaving. This is a terrible idea in and of itself, given that most non-security personnel do not regularly interact with inmates and are not familiar with their devious tactics. The likelihood of an inmate sneaking in with the visitors and leaving the institution unnoticed was high. The institution was fortunate in that no one anticipated the outcome, which left the inmates with minimal time to prepare and plot an escape.

Once all the guests had departed, the next stage of the chaos commenced. The majority of yard staff arrived slowly to assist in searching the inmates for contraband. Once there, the staff did minimal work, and as soon as the time was right, they swiftly departed unnoticed in the hopes of not having to do anything. Fortunately, I seized the opportunity to assist. I spent an extra two hours there searching inmates after the yard staff had already gone home. I never received a thank you for my assistance, a commendation for my excellent work, or even praise for my performance. Nope, nothing, just a big fuck you for helping out.

Don't lock me out

There is a limit to how much an officer can tolerate before they lose their composure and believe they have nothing left to lose. Screw the job, the benefits, and the vacation time—screw everything.

When an officer reaches that level, you would think management would intervene and prevent the officer from doing something stupid to save his career. After all, management preaches that we're family, and we have to look out for our brothers and sisters.

That is not always the case, as you will see in this story. The officer was on the unit, carrying out his duties, enforcing the rules as instructed, and holding offenders accountable.

An inmate, dissatisfied with his accountability, decided to take a stand. Instead of engaging in a verbal confrontation, the inmate waited until the officer was not looking before he threw his lock, striking him directly in the back. He thought the officer would call for backup and take him to segregation with no consequences other than time in the hole.

Oh no, that is not how it went down.

The officer, who was quite a large man, had had enough of the nonsense. Fuck everything and everyone. He unleashed a furious assault on the inmate.

The inmate knew immediately that he had made a mistake in his actions as the officer turned the inmate's face into a piece of pulverized meat, bone, and teeth. Had he known the officer's intentions, he may not have acted the way he did.

The officer persisted in physically assaulting the inmate from all angles. He only stopped when additional staff arrived and pulled him off, probably saving the inmate's life.

Medical personnel immediately took the inmate and determined that he needed to go to the hospital.

On the other hand, they planned to send the officer home.

To everyone's shock and horror, they put both the inmate and the officer together on the way out, where the inmate continued to run his mouth, provoking the officer.

Unable to resist, he attacked the inmate, forcing staff to

intervene, thereby saving his life. The inmate's restraint hindered his ability to defend himself, allowing the officer to deliver a forceful blow to his face.

Whoever in management thought that pairing those two would be acceptable should have immediately resigned. You never put an inmate and an officer together after a fight. To me, this was nothing more than a set-up by the institution to give them a reason to either make the officer quit or fire him.

Stolen vehicle

One would assume that the state would maintain a record of all its vehicles, maintenance, service history, and location. Unfortunately, this prison feels that's unnecessary information.

It all began with a man-down call and an inmate escort to the infirmary. After some time and diagnosis, the hospital decided the inmate needed to stay and admitted him.

The situation was much worse than originally expected, and the inmate was going to be there for a while. No harm, no foul. Right... wrong.

The way this works is that the initial medical trip leaves the vehicle at the hospital, just in case the inmate needs to return for an unknown reason. This approach eliminates the need for the institution to pick up the staff and inmate. The hospital watch relief brings a new vehicle, which is brought back by the staff getting off work. This ensures that a vehicle is always present at the hospital.

Days turned into months, and eventually the inmate was ready to return. The hospital staff contacted the institution, stating that they needed a vehicle to transport the inmate back. This situation defies logic, as they ought to have possessed a vehicle.

Without question, the institution sends another vehicle to the hospital to retrieve both the staff and the inmate. No one inquires about the other vehicle.

After a week or so, someone finally realizes the vehicle is missing, but due to the passage of time, they are unable to recall or identify the vehicle's owner. Having no other option, they presume it's a stolen vehicle, notify the police, and proceed with the report.

Three weeks later, the hospital calls the institution, asking if they are ever going to get the vehicle that has been parked there for months. Eventually, the institution towed the vehicle back due to its dead battery and informed the police about its discovery.

What's with the board

This might be common sense, or a lesson we've all learned in life: when you have a list of names to verify, you go through the list and mark each person off to ensure you have them all. This process is no different from that of shopping or managing a construction project. Given this knowledge, why is it so difficult for the lieutenants to ensure that everyone is present?

Here is a fine example. I'm waiting for my relief to come, and I continue to do so. Eventually, I realize that my relief is unlikely to arrive, so I decide to call control and inquire about who has the board.

With their name in hand, I begin my search for them. Once I locate the lieutenant, the conversation always starts with the same question: "Where are you?"

> **"The problem with incompetence is its inability to recognize itself." ~ Orrin Woodward.**

Where I'm at shouldn't matter; if they had everyone, I wouldn't be calling. Anyway, I explain which unit I'm on, and as normal, the

Incompetence is often highly regarded in governmental circles.

William Wallace

phone goes quiet as they look through the roster to see who my relief is.

And here we go with the excuses, which range from "He is coming from another unit and needed to take his lunch break" to "They should be here, and I don't know why they aren't." My favorite excuse was when I had to make a call and the lieutenant said, "Oh yeah, I don't remember them being in roll call."

Well, Jesus Christ, if you never saw them at roll call, why the hell didn't you have control call them at home and have yard staff relieve me?

Here's another scenario that I find inspiring. If I am ten minutes late, I am required to write a memo and request a leave of absence. If the lieutenant is unable to get me out on time due to their inability to manage the roster and ensure everyone is present, shouldn't they be required to write a memo explaining their incompetence at their job and their inability to ensure my timely departure? Working in corrections has taught me that management can do no wrong while the officers who do the work continually get fucked. Engaging in bitching, complaining, and paperwork may lead to perceptions of you as a nuisance, a complainer, or a problem.

"IF STRATEGIC INCOMPETENCE IS IDENTIFIED, SENIOR MANAGERS SHOULD HAVE A DIRECT AND HONEST CONVERSATION WITH THE EMPLOYEE INVOLVED. PROVIDE SPECIFIC EXAMPLES OF THEIR BEHAVIOR AND ITS IMPACT ON THE TEAM AND ORGANIZATION. EXPRESS EXPECTATIONS CLEARLY AND OFFER SUPPORT TO HELP THEM IMPROVE"

John Onyeukwu

Should be mandatory to understand this

Riding suit

> "Oh, what a tangled web we weave, when first we practice to deceive!"
>
> Sir Walter Scott

This case involves a lieutenant who had the opportunity to make the right decision but chose not to do so for unknown reasons.

The officer's job required him to leave his post, so whenever he had to leave, he always locked the door to protect his lunch box. In the past, there have been incidents where individuals have stolen and consumed someone else's food.

After finishing his checks, the officer was on his way back to his station when he noticed a sergeant in training trying to enter the building.

"What are you doing?" the officer asked.

The sergeant in training began to scream at the officer, "Open this fucking door!"

Once again, the officer inquired about his needs inside the building, given that it was unusual for the sergeant to enter it.

"I need to get in," the sergeant in training screamed.

"Nah, I'm good," the officer said.

"I need to do my fucking job." The sergeant in training was belligerent.

Immediately after he unlocked the door, the irate sergeant in training shoved the officer out of the way from behind.

The officer took the correct action by calling the lieutenant and informing him about the incident. During the conversation, the officer expressed concerns about potential serious harm to the sergeant in training if he were to repeat the same actions.

The lieutenant approached him and informed him that he would watch the camera, and if he lied, he would face immediate dismissal. He must have watched the video, realized its truth, and experienced a sudden change in attitude. Instead of telling the officer that he needed to write paperwork and send the other sergeant in training home for assault pending an investigation, he tried to bribe the officer by giving him a one-piece riding suit.

The officer declined the request because he didn't require one.

The lieutenant persisted in offering him the suit at no cost, stating that even if he declined, he could potentially sell it.

Again, the officer said no.

The lieutenant, for all intents and purposes, begged the officer not to report it, as he (the lieutenant) was already in hot water with the captain for an incident that happened earlier with another officer.

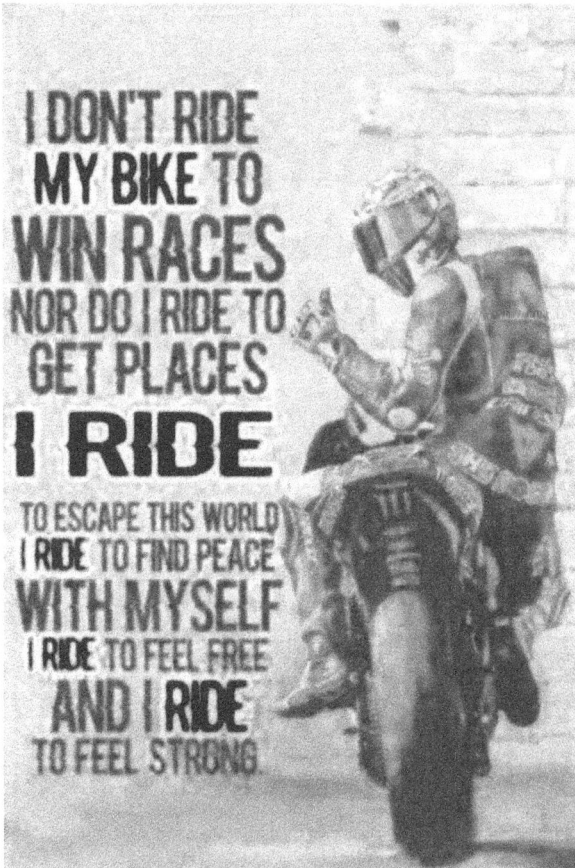

I DON'T RIDE MY BIKE TO WIN RACES NOR DO I RIDE TO GET PLACES I RIDE TO ESCAPE THIS WORLD I RIDE TO FIND PEACE WITH MYSELF I RIDE TO FEEL FREE AND I RIDE TO FEEL STRONG.

Zero pass down

I don't mean to be an asshole, but sometimes I look at people and think, That's the sperm that won. You can just see it in their eyes; the son of a bitch is lost.

There are no words in the dictionary that accurately describe how stupid this person is. I didn't use the word "dumb" because there is a distinction between the two. Dumb is doing something wrong, but not knowing it's wrong. Stupid is doing something wrong while knowing it's wrong.

clusterfuck

/klə-stər-fək/ noun

1. **complex, utterly disordered and mismanaged situation**
2. **a muddled mess**

Let me explain to you the situation, and then you can decide for yourself.

After a staff assault, a use of force, and a medical trip, the institution went into lockdown. Everything up till now sounds like SOP (standard operating procedures). Now is when things get fuzzy.

The captain who was in charge of the institution completely neglected to inform the next shift what had occurred. How is that even possible?

Management preaches to us about doing a proper pass down. Make sure the officer coming on knows exactly what is happening before you leave. So I ask this again. How could a captain be so incredibly incompetent as to remain silent?

This lack of information left the next shift unsure about whether to run their lines or not. The entire institution descended into chaos, with no one understanding what was going on. Despite their reputation for stability and communication, the organization failed miserably during one of the most crucial periods.

Code of silence

Every day, you, as correctional officers, encounter violence. You expect that from the inmates. At any given time, you anticipate receiving a blow to the head from behind. What you don't expect is violence or threats of violence from fellow staff. Unfortunately, we don't live in a perfect world and are sometimes subject to the stupidity of others.

This incident occurred one night in segregation when a rather large officer decided to vent his frustration on a female staff member who was so skinny that she had to run around in the shower to get wet.

It all began because of a chair—yes, a chair. The officer had to use the lieutenant's chair because it was the only one he could fit in.

The sergeant made that statement, "He's a big boy." Instead of saying that the officer's ass looked like 150 pounds of chewed bubble gum, the sergeant should have told him to go walk some laps around segregation.

I went to the doctor, and he said I was a beast. No fat ass, he said you were obese

As she walked up the stairs, the female officer joked, "That's why I always take the stairs."

The fat tub of shit rose to his feet in a combative stance, his fist clenched, and roared, "You want to go, you fucking bitch."

The female officer said nothing as she went to finish her checks. Upon her return, she requested a memo from the other staff members who were present during the verbal attack.

One would think you would expect more from the sergeants present, but alas, the code of silence and the good ol' boys run deep.

"It's us three against you, and they're not going to side with you," the lard ass bellowed.

One sergeant stated that, "I don't think he said that," while the other said, "I don't know if I heard that." What makes this whole thing worse is that the wife of one of the sergeants watches the officer's children.

Nepotism is alive and thriving

"Don't worry, I got your back, giving the boss's children Christmas presents or you want to golf this weekend. All of this is completely innocent and usually means nothing. Sometimes though, there can be ulterior motives and it falls under nepotism.

Nepotism is the practice of giving relatives or friends an unfair advantage, such as a job, promotion, or increased pay in the workplace. It's a form of favoritism that can occur in almost any industry and can have serious consequences for the company, including:

Demotivation:

Employees may feel that promotions and opportunities are based on personal relationships rather than merit, which can lead to low morale and frustration.

Loss of talent:

High-performing employees may leave the company in search of fairer opportunities.

Resentment:

Employees may feel unfairly treated, which can lead to a toxic work environment.

Erosion of trust:

When employees perceive that the workplace is characterized by favoritism, trust in leadership and management can erode.

Everyone in the business knows that nepotism happens. Because of this, the next question should be: Is nepotism legal, and the answer is no. Allow me to say this again. Nepotism is inherently not illegal in the workplace. There are no federal laws or statutes specifically prohibiting nepotism, but it can still result in discrimination, which is illegal in the workplace. More importantly than nepotism being illegal is the fact that nepotism can result in the creation of a hostile workplace. Recognizing and addressing these issues is crucial for maintaining a healthy, equitable work environment. The Department of Corrections understands this, and that is why they have developed policies forbidding nepotism. Still, somehow, nepotism thrives within the Department of Corrections. What we have in this section are all stories based off of nepotism, even though there are policies prohibiting its growth.

"Nepotism" is a polite way of saying
"you have no chance in hell of ever being promoted."

Not part of the system

From birth, for most people, we have ambitions to advance in whatever we do. After kindergarten, we move up to grade school, then middle school, and eventually high school. Some people enter the military, where they strive to promote up through the ranks—private, specialist, sergeant—all the way up to the top. For those who enter the workforce, their aspirations may differ, yet they remain consistent. They may begin their career on the loading dock, progress to the manager position, and eventually oversee the operation as the CEO.

Unfortunately, nepotism often crushes dreams and aspirations. In my experience, nepotism typically arises during the early stages of a career when individuals are attempting to progress, but I have also observed instances of it occurring later in life, once they have accumulated a significant amount of experience. For me, it started earlier in my career, and the advice I received has consistently proven accurate.

After completing my first year, I received a call from the lieutenant's office. I had never faced any problems, received no communication, received no written warnings, or experienced any discipline. I wondered what this was about as I exited the unit.

"Come in and have a seat," the lieutenant said.

Flopping down in the chair, I asked, "What's up?"

"You're here for your yearly review."

"Ah, okay."

Reaching inside her desk, she pulled out a sheet of paper, asked me questions about various aspects of the job, scribbled a few notes, and then slid the paper back into the drawer. What happened next left me astounded. She asked me what my plans were for working there.

I informed her that my aspiration was to become a counselor, as it aligns with my bachelor's degree.

She never missed a beat as she looked me right in the eye and spoke. "Even though you are more qualified than 90% of the counselors we have, it will never happen, as you are not part of the good old boy's system."

Her words struck a chord with me as I witnessed individuals

without experience receiving promotions for available positions. What they possessed was not experience or a college degree; it was nepotism. Their kids all played on the same baseball teams; they coached each other's kids, played football, and went to school together. If we had to tell each other, "Sorry, you didn't get the job because we had to give it to this outsider who knows nobody," how would we perceive it? They couldn't allow that to happen, so the best way to prevent it is to never let it begin.

What do you call an HR manager who only hires their friends?

A NEPOTISM ENTHUSIAST.

Physical plant fiasco

We all have dreams, aspirations, and the desire to advance in life. Some people choose to stay in the same profession their entire career, while others jump from job to job, never finding what they're looking for. Some people leave their jobs as they grow irritated with management and seek a different system. Some leave for reasons unknown. We do know that when an attractive job opens up in the same organization, many qualified applicants apply.

This was the case when the physical plant sent out a message they were accepting applications for not just one position, but three. Excitement was in the air, as the opportunity to leave corrections behind is rare, and the chances were now even better. The majority of staff, if not everybody, applied. During the night, there were whispers of optimism as individuals shared their experiences and reasons for applying for a job. Others accused them of not being sufficiently qualified, prompting people to defend themselves.

As the closing date neared, anxiety rose. Who would get the three positions? Who would win, and who would be upset? Rumors began to circulate, likely originating from the same individuals. The notification revealing the selection took an eternity to arrive, but when it did, cries of anger filled the institution. Grab your pitchforks and torches, charge the castle, and burn the place to the ground.

There lingered the question of why the employees were upset. Management refused to address the situation; they made the decision and stood by it with unwavering bravery.

The employees' anger stemmed from the fact that all three individuals chosen for the coveted positions had ties to individuals already employed in the physical plant. The nepotism was blatant, with uncles, nephews, and cousins being the least qualified candidates for any of the positions. The management failed to address the issue, which further strained relations between them and the employees.

They say time heals all wounds. I disagree. This wound never healed; it became infected and festered out of control. Even now, you can still hear the lonesome cries of those who experienced the great physical plant fiasco and felt mistreated. Since the results were as expected, I moved on.

J. R. Harris

Breaking
NEWS

The Haunting

Prisons and jails are often considered to be among the most haunted places in the United States. The trauma and suffering experienced at the hands of others leave a lasting impression, and all too often the spirits of the deceased choose to remain.

This officer was so horrified by his experience that he left the lights on and refused to work in the dark.

The night started like any other night, but right around 3ish in the morning he noticed a shadow near the end of the tier. He thought the sergeant was setting him up, so he called down to find out if they were teasing him.

The sergeant replied that he was not playing games, nor was anyone else. If you are not playing games, then there's an inmate at the end of the tier, and I am looking at him right now.

He immediately made his way to the unit, curious about the situation and how the inmate managed to escape from his cell.

Upon the sergeant's arrival, he noticed the officer standing in the officer's station, staring down the tier. Almost immediately, the sergeant approached the officer's station and noticed the shadow at the end of the tier. "Let's go find out who this is," the sergeant said, and the pair began their march down the tier.

When they were halfway down the tier, the shadow turned and walked directly through a closed and locked door.

For a moment they both stood there stunned with what they had seen.

The officer was having none of it and turned on all the lights on the unit, refusing to sit there in the dark.

Can you blame him?

I asked my wife if I was the only one she ever slept with?

She said yes, all the others were nines and tens.

Down with the dirty

You'd think the institution would listen to your input after years of experience. Oh no, not this place. This particular institution severely punishes anyone who speaks out, especially if the speech targets a family member of the management. I'm not sure if they planned to make an example out of this officer or humiliate him to the point he decided to quit. Either way, he stood firm on his resolution and, in the end, won.

The gist of the story is the officer saw the female employee doing some inappropriate things in the kitchen with the inmates. As he should have, he reported what he saw, and the entire management team turned against him. Make it known that this female employee was related to another member of management.

Due to his report, the officer faced severe consequences, including removal from his post and the placement of a letter of reprimand in his file.

Management should have immediately removed the female staff member from her post and placed her on leave for an investigation.

The officer was not allowed back into that area for any reason, and the way he was treated was simply disgusting.

Ultimately, the discovery of the female staff member engaging in sexual acts with the inmates and bringing in cell phones justified his actions.

The sad part of this story is that you would think management would bring the officer in and apologize for their actions. Oh no, that will never happen because those in management are also full-blown narcissists, and to admit they were wrong goes against every fiber of their being. They would rather die on the stake, set on fire, and burned to a crisp the entire time screaming how they did nothing wrong. Despite the officer's vindication for his role in reporting this, he faced significant challenges in removing the letter from his file.

How long is break

Some people find every way they can to get out of doing their job. The job of corrections is not that difficult, really; it isn't. The complexity lies in the intricacies that occur in the background. Let's take lunches and breaks, for example.

There should be two fifteen-minute breaks and one thirty-minute lunch break. Most people follow these rules, which ensures smooth operations. There is always someone who engages in some form of deception and attempts to gain an advantage.

What makes this particular story so damning is that the person assisting him in manipulating the system is a lieutenant.

You guessed it. Yes, they are related. In this particular case, the lieutenant covers for the officer, allowing them to take extra time for lunch and breaks.

If you asked the lieutenant why, they would give you every possible reason for your mistake. I firmly believe that management receives instructions on mastering the art of gaslighting rather than focusing on their duties. Trying to make you feel crazy while unzipping your pants to fuck you.

What I speak of is not hearsay information, as I have personally experienced it while offering this officer a break. He came back, and I asked him what the hell took so long. And he responded with, "I was just talking with _____ (intentionally left blank). I informed him that breaks were only fifteen minutes, not thirty, as I have two more breaks to do.

I talked with _____, and they covered for him, making every excuse. What they should have done was simply own up to their mistakes. However, this is unlikely to occur, as pure narcissism taints management, and admitting they are wrong can be catastrophic.

Gift wrapped promotions

There are certain requirements that must be met in order to be promoted; that is, unless you have family in high places. Only then do those requirements become irrelevant, stomped into the ground until they become pulverized, and then flushed down the drain with the family's own shit.

This just happened to be the case of one employee who promoted up through the ranks, giving no fucks about those who observed how bad he fucked the system.

The employee spent very little time as an officer, never worked in a housing unit, and was given every easy job. It must be comforting to have a high-ranking relative. Eventually he was promoted to an out-of-class sergeant well before the employee met the requirements.

After becoming a sergeant in training, he had his sights set on a higher position. Unbelievably, he never achieved the status of a permanent sergeant before receiving a promotion to lieutenant. This is where things turned fuzzy, as the job description stipulates that a sergeant must have at least one year of experience to be promoted to lieutenant. Despite never achieving permanent sergeant status, this officer received the lieutenant position. Yes, let me state that again. Despite being a sergeant in training, this employee received the promotion to lieutenant. Man, what a betrayal to the sergeants who endeavored to advance. I could only imagine the level of hate and anger of those who put in their time and ultimately failed.

The promotions didn't end there; they continued up through the ranks to captain, a position he didn't hold very long before receiving his next promotion.

It's sad when you witness the number of qualified candidates get turned down for a promotion due to an employee who is unqualified, yet has the support of family in high places. Great way to demoralize the staff who have put in their time, and prove that family really is thicker than experience.

Friends

Experts say that the pen is mightier than the sword. This may be true or not; I'm not an expert. What I do know is that the friend is mightier than the experienced. This may not sound logical, but you will understand before this story ends.

You see, the institution posted a job opening for a counselor position. Fantastic! That's exactly what I've been waiting for, as it aligns perfectly with my past. I should have known better, as I had been told in the past that I would never go anywhere because I was not part of the system. Regardless, I believed that mentality was in the past.

I fill out the application, cross every T, and dot every I. Send a beautiful resume with my experience, my education, and a full page of references. I mean this thing had the USDA stamp of approval. It was so good that it should have been hung on the wall of the Smithsonian as a perfect example for all others to follow.

I continue to wait, but nothing happens. Weeks go by, and still nothing. How is this even possible? I ask myself.

Eventually, the email arrives, extending a hearty congratulations to _____. I almost shit my pants when I read the name. How is that even possible? They lack experience, for heaven's sake. I reread the email thinking this has to be a joke. Nope, no joke. They chose someone for this position with no experience over someone who has a bachelor's degree in criminal justice and an associate's degree in psychology.

Then it came to me like a gift from heaven. I gazed into the icy, clear waters of a fountain of tears, and a vision materialized, supplying me with the essential understanding.

I remember now that the current counselors and this individual were all friends. They went to lunch together, hung out at the company softball games, and, let's not forget, they probably also had sexual relations with each other's husbands.

Needless to say, I watched the potential job go up in smoke, and it was then the words came back to me. "You will never go anywhere because you are not part of the system." God damn, she was right.

HOW "SELF-MADE" BILLIONAIRES GOT THEIR START

Mom sat on the same board as the CEO of IBM and convinced him to take a risk on her son's new company

Started Amazon with $300,000 in seed capital from his parents and more from some rich friends

The son of a powerful congressman who owned an investment company

Dad owned an emerald mine in apartheid South Africa

Fired and rehired

Many things in life confuse me. I'm not perfect; I don't know everything, and I'm no expert on anything. I simply manage to make ends meet. What I do know is that when someone is severely abusing the system, there always seems to be nepotism behind it.

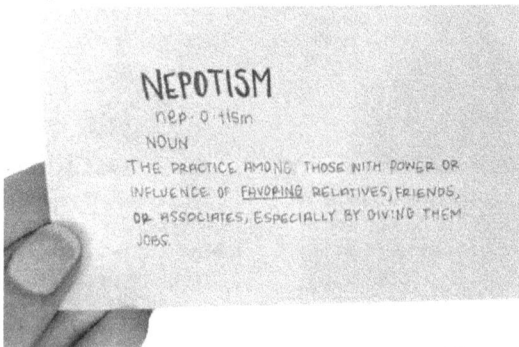

This is a perfect example of management taking advantage of the system. There was a female employee who worked in a different department that was walked out of the institution and not allowed on any state property. They fired her for arguing with management, talking behind their backs, and being a royal pain in the ass.

All of us who worked in the institution wondered what was going to happen next as she was married to an individual in upper management.

The outcome was exactly as anticipated. Within a week, she resumed her job, this time working under her husband's supervision. How in the hell is this even legal? Eventually, she transitioned to a different role, but her previous position abruptly vanished.

I understand family looks out for family. I get it; trust me, I do. Where it gets muddy is why has the same opportunity not been provided to officers in the past who have been fired? Why didn't the institution offer them a position in a different department?

The fact that management doesn't hide nepotism makes it sadder. They don't act in secret. Oh, no. They do it directly in your face, rubbing it in your nose and daring you to say anything about it, knowing that if you do, you're fucked.

Box of rocks

I wish someone could explain this to me like I'm a two-year-old. How is it possible for someone who is so stupid, they probably have to have Velcro straps on their shoes because they cant tie them, get promoted to sergeant.

Every time I have worked with this sergeant all he does is ask staff questions on how things operate and what needs to be done.

If you look deeper into the scenario, you will understand how this promotion came to fruition. Even though he does not have family in the business, it seems he married into it which qualifies him just the same.

Here is where it gets even worse, besides being dumb as a box of rocks, and being here for less than two years, he put in for a lieutenant's position that came open and got an interview.

THE RESULTS ARE IN AND YOU ARE DUMBER THAN A BOX OF ROCKS!

Not only did he survive the first interview, he got a second.

HOLY SHIT.

God damn it must be nice to be able to ride on the coat tails of management. They say the cream floats to the top. I hate to say this, but so does a big fat turd.

Good dude

How is it that some people get special favors, while others get fucked? We see it daily in all walks of life, but it seems more common in corrections. In this story, an officer faced termination due to dishonesty about a DWI, only to regain his job and privileges. Meanwhile, other staff members experienced a sense of betrayal akin to being fucked by a freight train.

A few years after his firing, the officer in question returned to work. His rehire allowed him to hold sergeant and segregation posts. You cannot do that until you have completed at least one year of service.

Frustrated by this, an officer contacted HR to inquire about his authorization to work in these positions despite not meeting the necessary qualifications. HR informed the officer that management had authorized it.

The officer persisted in his pursuit of justice, reaching out to the accountable manager to inquire about the officer and why he was allowed to work these posts when the officer does not meet the qualifications.

The manager responded that he grew up with this officer and that he is a *GOOD DUDE*. He went on to say that he grew up with this officer and that he used to work here, so the manager felt that the officer knew what he was doing.

This infuriated the officer even more, as he had an issue in the past and was supposed to be reinstated as if nothing occurred, but he was denied access to segregation.

It doesn't matter if this officer was his son. The fact remains that we must adhere to the established rules, policies, and procedures. To allow this individual to pass all the checks and balances just because he is a *"GOOD DUDE"* is just wrong.

Questioning management didn't accomplish anything, as the officer was allowed to continue working the post, while others were denied.

Scapegoat

Explain this to me like I am a six-year-old. What allows management to assign an officer to an out-of-control unit and expect them to take control in an hour?

This officer is attempting to manage the unit, operate the showers, and perform numerous other tasks simultaneously to restore order to the unit. During that period, a fight breaks out within a cell, leading to the stabbing of an inmate.

Management must be naive to believe that a single individual on a unit where the officer is occupied will notice this. This could have happened to anybody, and it probably has in the past, but they need to put the blame somewhere.

Meanwhile, the officer gets the unit organized and passes it on to the next shift. Only later in the evening, following the count, does the officer notice a problem. Believing himself to be an expert in drugs, the officer asserts that the inmate is under the influence of drugs, leading him to conclude that the inmate needs to go to segregation.

Two staff literally have to drag the inmate to segregation, where he is placed in a holding cell for forty-five minutes before medical finally arrives to assess the inmate, and that is when the stabbing is noticed.

Staff transport the inmate to the hospital per medical's recommendation.

You might be wondering why I've included this story in the nepotism section. Please allow me to explain.

The investigation focused on all those involved in the incident, except for one officer. This officer was the one who overlooked the inmate's distress during the count process. It was this officer who concluded that the inmate was under drug influence and warranted segregation. The officer has been in the institution for just over a year. It's worth noting that the officer who escaped investigation was the son of a lieutenant. The son of the lieutenant should have been the first one under investigation, given his failure to recognize the inmate's distress during a routine check to ensure the inmate is alive and well. Despite not being an expert, the lieutenant's son believed the inmate was on drugs. The lieutenant's son ordered the inmate to segregation instead of a nurse or the shift sergeant.

It seems to me that the institution is more interested in finding a scapegoat than in punishing the individual who was actually responsible for the incident.

"Sending Out the Scapegoat" by William James Webb

Membership has its privileges

We dedicate this section to all the "behind the scenes work," wink-wink, involved with corrections. You know, the extracurricular activity. If you're still confused, let me spell it out. The section focuses on S.E.X. in the workplace.

While there are no explicit rules, policies, or procedures prohibiting staff-on-staff relationships, I strongly discourage them. Throughout my tenure here, I have learned a few things along the way.

It is extremely easy for staff-on-staff relationships to begin even when one or both parties are married. This is because you spend a great deal of time working together, usually more time than you spend at home with your spouse. This situation arises due to the significant amount of overtime required for corrections. To pass the long days more quickly, some individuals engage in flirtatious behavior, which eventually develops into a relationship.

Another important thing to remember is that there are no secrets in prisons when it comes to relationships. If you do engage in an affair, prepare for the consequences, as the other half will discover it. I have never heard of an affair going on without the other partner finding out... ever.

For those who cheat thinking they found their soul mate, yeah, right. Hardly ever will anything serious come from an illicit relationship. When things go wrong and you have to work together, it can get tricky. Do you want the whole institution to know what you are like in bed? When you break up, everyone in the institution will know that you only have one nut (story included). Anyway, I'm not saying you can't have an affair; just be ready to face the repercussions of your choices, as these stories will demonstrate.

J. R. Harris

A man returning home a day early from a business trip got into the taxi at the airport.

It was after midnight. While en-route to his home, he asks the cabby if he would be a witness. The man suspected his wife was having an affair and he intended to catch her in the act.

For 100 dollars, the cabby agrees.

Quietly arriving at the house, the husband and cabby tiptoe into the bedroom.

The husband switched on the lights, yanked the blanket back and there was his wife in bed with another man.

The husband put a gun to the naked man's head.

The wife shouted, "don't do it." This man has been very generous! I lied when I told you I inherited money. He paid for the corvette I bought you. He paid for out new cabin cruiser. He paid for our house at the lake. He paid for our country club membership, and he even pays the monthly dues."

Shaking his head from side-to-side the husband slowly lowered the gun.

He looked over at the cab driver and said, "What should I do?"

The cabby said, "I'd cover his ass back up with that blanket before he catches a cold."

Ring don't plug a hole

It seems to me that the higher you go in corrections, the less moral, ethical, and value-driven you are. You expect new, younger staff to play around, but they eventually grow out of those activities as they age. That is not the case in corrections. In corrections, it appears that individuals become more daring in their ethical transgressions as they age. Some individuals not only transgress the boundaries of decency but also destroy any possibility of reconciliation. This just so happens to be one of those stories.

One thing you would not expect from a captain is to destroy a relationship, but that's exactly what happened.

The officer had a long day, worn out from dealing with the bullshit inside the institution, and just wanted to go home and relax. As he drove home, he dreamed of sipping an ice-cold beer, relaxing in his recliner, watching the game, and letting the day's problems fade away.

The reality of what happened was much different.

The officer arrived home and walked through the front door only to stare disaster straight in the face. A captain at the institution where he worked was kicking back in his favorite recliner, wearing his robe, and a musky, humid, swampy scent lingered on the air with slight traces of a woman's arousal. Only dirty feet, an unwashed beaver, and disappointment could create such a vile scent. Just when you think it couldn't get worse, it did. The captain was drinking the ice-cold beer that the officer bought. "Oh, hi, how are you doing?" the captain said as he sat there.

No words can describe the officer's anger at that moment. Thoughts of murder, revenge, hatred, betrayal, torture, and murder raced through his mind.

Luckily, the officer did the smart thing and just turned and walked away. A woman is not worth going to prison for, as there are plenty of other women out there who are clearly more faithful. Just remember, if a man steals your woman, the greatest gift is to let him keep her, as you are better off without her because real women don't cheat.

Laughter rocks

There's a lady who is cheating on her husband. One day while they are having sex, she hears her husband pull into the driveway. Her boyfriend says, "Oh no! What should we do?!" She says, "Hurry! Get dressed and go to the living room!" Once they're in the living room, she starts sprinkling baby powder all over him. He says, "What are you doing?" She says, "I'm making you white like a statue. Just stand in a pose; my husband will never know you're real, because he's stupid!" Her husband comes in and sees them and says to her, "What's that?" She says, "Well, Mrs. Johnson next door and I went shopping today. She has one just like it. I liked hers so much that she took me to get one." He shrugs it off and goes about his business. That night the boyfriend is still standing in the living room, still posed, too afraid to escape. He hears the husband wake up and open the bedroom door. The husband walks past him, opens the fridge, pops open a beer, and makes a bologna sandwich. He then walks up to the boyfriend and hands him the beer and sandwich and says, "Here, I was next door at Mrs. Johnson's house, stuck in that position for 2 days, and no one gave me anything to eat."

Night out

We all want to help a co-worker whenever possible. Some co-workers take it to the next level and leave you shocked. Unsure what to say, you stand there debating if you should walk away or kick them in the nuts.

This is the case of a co-worker who was single, kind of shy, very ugly (according to my wife), found it hard to talk to the ladies, and somewhat of an introvert. Doing my duties as a friend, I invited him out to a night of bowling with me and my wife. My wife was bringing a co-worker as well in hopes that they would meet up. Well, it turned out that the girl my wife brought had no interest in the man, so we decided to go to a club in the same building. I thought perhaps there I could find him a date.

We arrive at the club just as things are kicking off. I have no issues talking to women, so I begin my search for the perfect date. Locating two women at the bar, I tell him to follow me. It doesn't take me long, and soon I have them both out on the dance floor. While out there, I explain that I am married but trying to help my friend find someone, as he is quite shy. I turn around to introduce my co-worker, and he is gone. I spot him sitting alone at the table

I head back to the table and ask him what the fuck happened. He responded that those were not my type of women. I sigh, okay, what kind are you looking for.

He looks around the bar and points to a lady standing by the door in a security uniform. "Now she is my type of woman," he says.

Mission accepted, I thought, and then I depart. My eyes were on the target the entire time, like a panther on the hunt. I move in for the kill and introduce myself. We hit it off right off the bat, and we chat for a good ten minutes. It was then that I explained the situation. I'm here trying to find a friend, a girl... blah, blah, blah. You know the routine.

She asked where he was sitting. I point him out, and she goes over and introduces herself. I lose interest in the situation and begin to spend time with the wife. We're dancing and having a good time. An hour must have passed, and I see him sitting alone again. She is once again back by the door, so I go and ask her how it went. She explained to me that they talked for a bit, but he is a loser, and she lost interest.

We stayed for a few more hours, and the night was ending. I was done searching because the local prospects were thinning. Women were more interested in getting home now and not looking for a partner. As me and the wife were getting ready ourselves, he asked what we were going to do now. I responded with going home. To my shock and horror, he offered to come home with us. Before I could speak, he asked if we were interested in a threesome. I stood there flabbergasted that a co-worker would bluntly ask such a question. We're supposed to be buddies, co-workers, friends, not applying for a porno position. It was then I started distancing myself from him.

How come all women love Jesus?

Because he's hung like this.

Dirty little secrets

In the world of corrections, you hear some of the craziest shit. Sometimes you hear it directly, and other times it filters up through the grapevine. When it comes through the grapevine, you tend to question its legitimacy. Face-to-face, no-questions-asked situations often leave you stunned by the audacity of some people.

One such incident occurred in my dayroom. She came to offer me a break, and a conversation ensued about relationships outside of the marriage. Why this happened, I'm not sure. Perhaps she was testing me or looking for justification for her own action.

She revealed to me during our conversation that it was okay for a woman to cheat on her husband as long as he doesn't know.

I stood there, eyes wide and mouth agape. How is this mentality even feasible? I asked her to continue.

She clarified that as long as he remained unaware of the affair, there was no harm.

I asked if it was mutual. Is it acceptable for him to have an affair with another girl, provided she remains unaware?

She just about blew a gasket as she came unglued. "If he ever fucked another woman, I would beat his ass, divorce him, and take everything with me."

"So, this is essentially a one-way road. You can go out and screw around, but it's not okay for him. How is this even okay?"

She just said she had more breaks to do and swiftly departed. I think I hit a nerve, or the reality of the situation hit home. Perhaps she was worried that I would tell her husband, even though I had never met him.

All in the family

This story is short, sweat, and straight to the point. There is no need to embellish it or string the reader along. The brutality of it all warrants such actions.

Even though this story falls under the "membership has its privileges" chapter, nepotism also plays a significant role. You see, when you use your positions to land family members their jobs, sometimes, their actions on the job return a slap with the force of a thousand dead pimps.

This is the story of a high-ranking member of management who used

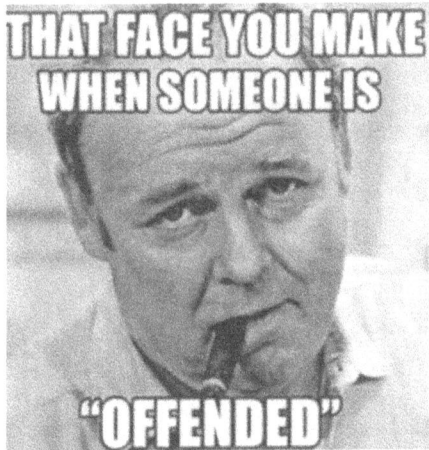

THAT FACE YOU MAKE WHEN SOMEONE IS "OFFENDED"

his position to land his wife and his daughter jobs that neither were fit for.

We'll begin with the daughter, as hers is a simple story. She was caught fucking an inmate. Plain and simple. No other way to slice it.

On the other hand, the wife's story goes much deeper. You see, the husband persistently reported to other officers that their wives were cheating on them, solely for the purpose of causing trouble and discontentment. As it turns out, his wife was actually cheating on him with his best friend, who also worked at the prison.

Before her eventual dismissal, she visited another unit to bid farewell to an inmate. There is no proof of this, but the story goes that she was in his cell for over an hour before she left. I wonder what was going on in his cell during that time.

The husband, distraught from all that occurred, attempted to take his own life.

Lip-smacking good

Going through the training to become a correctional officer, you form a special bond with those around you. This usually occurs because you don't know anyone else, and everyone is facing the same challenges. It's not uncommon for a group to hang out after work, head to a bar, play some pool, and enjoy a few drinks. This narrative recounts the events that transpired that evening at the bar as the training was nearing its conclusion.

One week remained before we graduated and went our own way. A few officers decided that holding a gathering at the bar would be an excellent way to end training. We all met at the bar around 7ish. Some people were doing shots in celebration; others just nursed a beer. As for me, I abstained from alcohol due to a troubled past. It was nothing extravagant, just a group of people enjoying each other's company. As the night drew to a close, a married female officer wrapped her arms around me and planted a kiss on my neck.

I was shocked and didn't know what to say. I just stood there frozen.

"Did you want to come back to my place?" she asked.

"Uh, aren't you married?" I asked.

"Yes, I am, but my husband is gone," she whispered.

I politely declined the invitation, letting her know that I was married and didn't think such behavior was acceptable.

"I understand," she said before kissing me again. No harm, no foul, I guess.

As we left, I saw another officer getting into her vehicle. I guess she was determined to get what she wanted, regardless of the consequences of her actions. To this day I still don't know if her husband ever found out.

Horse D

Men are often accused of having dirty mouths. I, for one, would have to disagree. I would argue that women can be just as impure, if not more so. Every one of us has encountered a friend who suddenly says something so outrageous that it leaves you stunned. This was the case with a female friend of mine who decided to share her story.

My friend arrived around the middle of the shift to engage in casual conversation and pass the time. Looking back, I believe it was more to brag than anything else.

Well, anyway, and don't ask me how we got on the subject of her latest fling, even though she is married, which I brought to her attention, but she and her husband were currently in a tiff and broken up, she explained.

To my surprise, she informed me of the last person to give her the bone.

I was taken aback when she even mentioned it, but now the secret was revealed. I had no choice but to wait for her to finish.

She continued to explain how this man had a monster of a meat stick. She attempted to demonstrate the girth of this club with her fist, which shocked and horrified me.

You couldn't stop staring at her; it was like witnessing a catastrophic train accident.

She continued to explain that when he finally managed to sink the submarine, he could not fit the entirety of this Alabama black snake inside her.

I was appalled by what I was hearing and assumed she must be lying, but who am I to judge? With nothing left to say, I said the only thing I could think of. "Where was your husband during all this?"

This was the most distressing aspect of the entire ordeal. It was not the size of his junk, not how she was married, not where it happened, but the worst part was that her husband was downstairs watching TV while she was upstairs getting pounded like the only drum at an all-day rock concert.

Apology accepted

We've all heard a saying in this world before. The saying is, "Never dip your pen in the company inkwell." To put it another way, the phrase "don't get your honey where you make your money" applies. To break it down even further, it's an explanation to not hook up with anyone at work, as it produces nothing but problems.

This narrative recounts the tale of a married lieutenant who, despite his marital status, believed it would be beneficial for him to dip his pen in the company ink. Most people knew the affair was happening regardless of how many times they tried to deny it.

I really didn't care because it didn't affect me. As adults, those two have the freedom to act as they please, and if they decide to end their marriages, that's their choice. As time went on, the lieutenant's performance at his job deteriorated, often neglecting his duties to spend more time with his fling.

Instead of staying in his office, he would go out to the mobile and ride around the institution for hours with her, forgetting he still had a job inside.

Eventually, we needed to address his poor performance, and I was the right person to handle it. When another officer entered the unit to give me a break, I lost my composure. After I yelled and screamed about his shitty work performance, I told the officer that the lieutenant needs to lay off the drugs or stop fucking her.

The officer argued back, saying that he does not know what is wrong with us and why we are accusing the lieutenant of this. "The lieutenant and she are not having an affair, and he didn't know the motive behind our actions," he said.

I argued back that it was true, and if he didn't like it, then that was on him.

A few weeks later, the affair came to light, revealing that the lieutenant was indeed having an affair. This revelation led to his removal from his position. I was standing outside the roll call when the officer approached me. He said that he wanted to apologize and that he didn't think the lieutenant would be like that.

I said that I believed it was painfully obvious, but I accepted his apology, and all is good.

Todays bonus – Strange noises –

The night started like any other, dull and boring. As time passed, the officer decided to do a check to make sure the inmates were not participating in any illegal activity.

Partway down the hall, she heard some strange noises coming from a room where there are no inmates allowed, nor should there be officers in there.

Having no key to enter the room, she did the next best thing and kneeled down on the floor to look under the door to see what the hell was going on. The noise continued to mimic the sound of furniture sliding across the floor.

Unable to see anything, she returned to the officer's station and waited.

The noises continued for a bit longer, then a sergeant and an officer exited the room and entered the hallway.

She asked them what they were doing, and the sergeant made the statement that they were doing searches.

Why in the hell would the sergeant be doing searches in an area where inmates don't go? And why would the sergeant be doing searches anyway? It seems to me that there was some extra-curricular activity occurring in that room that night, and it wasn't searches.

joke of the day

My brother was murdered today.

Officer: "Do you mind identifying the body, I have to warn you the body was hacked up."
Me: "Yes that's my brother Reese."
Officer: "You're sure?"
Me: "Yup, those are Reese's Pieces."

What's in a picture

In the past, I often arrived twenty to thirty minutes early and spent time in the muster room. Drink a soda, eat a snack, or just bullshit with the other staff that were already there. How could I have known that today would be a day of change? As I enter the muster room, I notice the shift lieutenant seated at a desk, with a senior male officer on either side, staring blankly at a plain white sheet of paper. Thinking nothing of it, I check my mailbox, then turn and ask, What's so exciting?

The shift lieutenant waves me over and shows me the page with the pictures of three new female staff members on it.

"What's up with them?" I ask.

"We're debating which ones we're going to try and score with," the shift lieutenant responds.

"Are you shitting me?" I asked. "And by the way, aren't you married?"

The shift lieutenant points at one of the pictures (I think the left one) and mentions being cute.

I inquired about the shift lieutenant's marital status once more, but he never responded. In the meantime, the other two officers started chatting among themselves about the remaining women on the list.

Seeing that I was getting nowhere and feeling somewhat disgusted with the entire situation, I decided to leave the area and take a seat at a different table.

About this time, a senior female officer entered the muster room and asked, "What's up?"

I responded, "Oh, they're just looking at the new female staff that they're going to try and bang."

The look she gave them pierced each of their souls with fear, and you could sense the panic that set in.

"We are not," the shift lieutenant screamed as he crumbled up the page. "Why would you even say anything like that?" he continued as he tossed the page in the garbage.

The two officers gave me a piercing glance before departing.

The senior female officer shook her head in disgust, then departed as if the behavior was inappropriate but tolerated after years of abuse.

We sat staring at each other with tension thicker than London fog. It only cleared once the rest of the night shift staff began to trickle into the muster room.

Extra story

Actions have consequences, and the game shows no mercy. If you aspire to be a hoe, regardless of gender, express your intentions clearly. When you try to keep your personal life secret while screwing coworkers, prepare for the consequences.

This is precisely the situation this officer found herself in after having an affair with a co-worker. Her husband divorced her, and the officer with whom she had the affair was not interested in a long-term relationship, thus ending things almost immediately.

Enter the next smooth-talking gigolo, and she found herself involved in another relationship that she thought meant something. Oh no, the game doesn't play that way. The officer, like the other, wanted to immerse his sub in her after hearing she was good in the sack.

Word spread like a dry brush fire that she was easy, and officers, married or not, lined up to try and get some. A few officers succeeded, but their relationships always ended the same way, with the other officers not interested in something long-term. Meanwhile, depression crept in and her mental state deteriorated.

As time passed, she sunk deeper into depression until one day, she failed to show up for work and never answered her phone. The next day she again was a no-show at work. A few days later, authorities found her on her couch, suffering from a self-inflicted gunshot wound to the head. What's even worse is that she had two younger children who were there with the body.

Inmates need loving too

Officer and inmate relationships are considered illegal, even if they're consensual. This is because the power dynamic between COs and inmates is such that any sexual relations between them automatically constitute sexual abuse. A 2009 report from the Department of Justice states, "Under the federal criminal code, a prisoner's consent is never a legal defense due to the inherent unequal positions of prisoners and correctional and law enforcement staff who control many aspects of prisoners' lives."

Anybody with half a brain knows it's illegal to have a sexual relationship with an inmate. The academy teaches us this. Every year, we conduct training with PREA, which explains this to us; we have staff available to assist if something inappropriate arises and you're not sure which way to turn. However, we are increasingly aware of the growing number of inmate relationships within correctional facilities. This is just one example among many, and it has had a devastating impact on three careers.

Within the first year of their career, the officer established a relationship with a married colleague. This alone should shed light on the officer's mindset. She doesn't care about the other person involved; in her mind, it's all about her.

As time passed, rumors began to circulate that she was also involved with an inmate. The rumor was that at 11:00 pm she would slip into the cell and spend time with her inmate friend. I am not aware of what transpired inside that cell, but I am certain that it was something illegal. Regardless, I cannot confirm the accuracy of the information, as I do not conduct investigations. However, I'm confident that the investigation department was thoroughly investigating the matter. One day she was just gone, and then the story broke wide open. Not only was the officer found guilty of being involved with an inmate, she was also bringing in drugs and cell phones. When presented with the evidence, she resigned from her position before they had a chance to fire her.

Unfortunately, the other officer who she was dating eventually separated from his wife and divorced. There were rumors that he was also accused of introducing drugs into a secure facility. I cannot be certain of this, as I am not an investigator; I can only report on what I see and hear. The institution no longer employs him, as far as I am aware.

The fiasco also involved his friend, with whom he hung out. Again, I am not privy to the evidence that implicated him, but there must have been something, given that he is no longer employed by the institution.

Three officers ultimately lost their jobs as a result of one female officer's decision to have a relationship with an inmate.

A farmer goes out and buys a new, young rooster. As soon as he brings him home, the young rooster rushes and screws all 150 of the farmer's hens. The farmer is impressed. At lunchtime, the young rooster again screws all 150 hens. The farmer is not just impressed anymore, he is worried. Next morning, not only is the rooster screwing the hens, but he is screwing the turkeys, ducks, and even the cow. Later, the farmer looks out into the barnyard and finds the rooster stretched out, limp as a rag, his eyes closed, dead, and vultures circling overhead. The farmer runs out, looks down at the young rooster's limp body and says: "You deserved it, you horny bastard!" And the young rooster opens one eye, points up at the vultures with his wing, and says, "Shhhh!, they are about to land."

???

I have 1001 questions about this story, and they all begin with what the fuck.

I'm not extremely religious, but I do believe this to be true. For most people, marriage is sacred and special in God's eyes! When two people get married, they become one, and God wants them to remain that way. Scripture says, "What God has joined let no man separate." God sees your marriage as special; the union you share with your spouse is important and precious to Him.

Some people do not view marriage this way. In fact, to them, marriage is nothing more than a piece of paper allowing you to receive benefits you might not otherwise get. Some people begin marriage with good intentions and then get drawn to another by looks or money. Some cheat on spouses without explanation. This just happens to be one of those cases.

This officer had an attractive wife, a few children, a home, and the appearance of a typical American family.

Indeed, his life was fulfilling until he realized there were better opportunities elsewhere. Yes, the officer had an affair. What made it even worse was he cheated on his wife with a coworker at the prison. Furthermore, he couldn't have chosen a more unattractive partner. He had to be either drunk or stoned to ruin your marriage over that thing, my God. No one is that stupid when they are sober.

I ran into him one day and asked him why; all he could do was shake his head and say, "I don't know."

Regardless, his wife found out about the affair and kicked his ass to the curb. I would expect nothing less from a decent woman, as taking him back in would be a slap in the face to her. She's better than that, and she deserves better.

So what does he do? He goes back to the beast he slept with and asks if he can move in. Either he was not that talented, or she simply used him as a toy because she told him to "fuck off," and he was unable to reside there. Besides, how would she explain it to her husband when there is another man sleeping in their bed? I would relish the opportunity to observe this situation firsthand.

Having no other option, he reaches out to one of his friends and ends up living in his friend's basement.

See, pussy is a terrible thing. It will take you from the highest highs to the lowest lows, leaving you a broken and destroyed man living in a dumpster and fighting stray dogs for cold french fries.

THERE AIN'T NO WAY TO HIDE

YOUR LYING EYES...

Lies, damn lies, and management

There is no doubt that many people who work in the field of corrections lie. What makes the difference is who's telling the lie. If management catches an officer lying, it's likely they'll lose their job, as the first action they take is to bring up the ethics policy. When management lies, there is little to no punishment available. If you do question them, we are told that we are not allowed to do investigations. If you approach their supervisor, it's likely that no action will be taken, as they likely lied to secure their position. If you approach their supervisor, they will likely write you up for not adhering to the established hierarchy. If you escalate your concerns to the top, they will place you on paid leave while they investigate you, hoping to eliminate you before their hidden agendas become public.

One reason management is especially prone to lying is to maintain a positive reputation with subordinates, peers, and friends. Moreover, many managers derive a high degree of their own self-worth from their job performance. Many consider covering up mistakes with a few small lies or lying through omission as acceptable behavior, given the alternatives. Many believe that the benefits outweigh the costs. Managers are particularly susceptible to lying since they have more at stake financially and are not willing to give up their title or the trappings that their life and position may provide.

Throughout my tenure, I have noticed that most lies from management fall into one of these five categories.

1. **Create positive impression** – Everyone wants to project a positive image to others. Lies to create a good impression often comes in the form of exaggerated claims. One of the most common forms of lying to create a positive impression is when a person embellishes their accomplishments.

2. **Exercise power over others** – One way a liar can exercise their power over others is by controlling or falsifying the information another person has. Sometimes these lies may be false

information provided to the other party to make them go down a wrong path other times it may be through the omission of necessary information.

3. **Avoid embarrassment** – Lying to avoid being embarrassed will often be a lie of omission, such as claiming that they never read the email you sent. This type of lie also might include telling someone that their presentation was good- even when it sucked.

4. **Protect someone** – Perhaps one of the most common forms of lying is to protect another person because such an act makes one feel more justified in this type of lie. An example of a lie to protect another person is to provide the other person with a false alibi so that they do not get into trouble or get punished.

5. **Get out of awkward situations** – Many social situations can be awkward and people often will make up false excuses to avoid awkward conversations. For example, a manager might say that they have an important meeting they have to be at and cannot talk long when you have a complaint.

The bucket never lies

One would think working your ass off for the institution would get you somewhere, but all too often that is not the case. In the business of corrections, when the supervisor's witness you are doing a lot of overtime, helping out, or going the extra mile they come to expect it. On the one occasion you are burnt out, exhausted, or just plain lost interest, they turn on you.

I entered the roll call room to check in for my shift. At a far table, the lieutenant sat with the board flipping through some pages. Glancing up from the page, he saw me putting on my duty belt. "You want some overtime in the morning?" he asked.

"No, thank you," I replied. "I'm exhausted. I've worked the last three days. The only way I will stay now is if I get mandated."

"I got some easy overtime. Are you sure?"

"I'm positive," I responded.

Roll call finished, and I left for my unit. Once there, I checked the bucket list to see how many people were ahead of me. One, two, three... all the way up to six I counted, so I knew I should have been good.

The sergeant and lieutenant arrived about four in the morning to sign the logbook. It was then the lieutenant asked me again if I wanted to work some overtime. I explained to him again that I had no desire to work overtime. I was tired and was ready to go home and get some sleep. We chatted for a few minutes, then the lieutenant said. "Well, you go home and get some sleep, and I will see you tomorrow."

Once again, I thought that was the end of it until about seven in the morning when the phone rang. It was the lieutenant on the other end telling me that I was now stuck. I just about shit my pants when I asked him if he was sure. He responded with, "Yup, I just took a bunch of phone calls." He asked me if I wanted a unit or the yard to work. I took the yard as I knew I would get out sooner.

After a bit, I looked through the bucket list and began to call other staff who were ahead of me in the bucket to see where they got stuck. To my shock and horror, not one person ahead of me had even been called for overtime. I lost my shit knowing that the lieutenant had jumped over six people to make sure I got mandated.

As the day passed and I got more pissed, I wrote a memo to the superintendent explaining my displeasure with what had occurred. I explained how he straight-lied to me and how he jumped over the other staff to target me.

The next day I had a meeting with the superintendent, and he allowed me to read the lieutenants response to my memo. In his memo, he stated that, "I don't know why Harris is so pissed; he told me that he wanted the overtime." I told the superintendent that was a bold-faced lie and that he could ask the sergeant who was with us that night. He would verify that I told the lieutenant that the only way I was working was if I got mandated. If he ever did or not, I am not privy to it, but I can assure you, it put a damper on our working relationship as the trust had been shattered.

THE OLDER I GET
THE LESS
"LIFE IN PRISON"
IS A DETERRENT

Last in, first out, yeah right

It doesn't matter where you work as a correctional officer. Everywhere from California to North Carolina... Washington to Florida. From the farthest reaches of Alaska to the dry deserts of Arizona, overtime is in abundance. What matters is how that overtime is controlled. Each state seems to have its own unique system, and if you're the one who has to work it, it's never perfect.

In one state, the overtime is handled differently depending on which institution you work at. They employ a method commonly known as the bucket system. It's pretty simple and straightforward to follow. When the lieutenant needs to fill positions, he gives a mandate to the first person in line to stay and notifies the next person in line that they are in the bucket. If he gets mandated, then the next person in line is placed in the bucket. It goes on and on until the end of the shift or until every spot to run the institution is filled.

When it is time to get relieved. The last mandated person leaves first. It works on a last in, first out basis until the first person mandated gets out last. The union contract also stipulates this, so management should never question the process.

However, the issue arises when the lieutenant deviates from the established procedure and fails to follow it.

This story is short, but the message is extreme. One person was mandated twice near the bucket's end and should have been first out. Nope, that's not how it worked. He was the last one to leave both times. The first time it happened, he allowed it to slide. On the second occasion, he confronted the lieutenant, questioning why she had fucked him twice already.

The captain confronted him and chastised him for interrogating the lieutenant. The captain explained that the lieutenant was tired from working overtime... well, fuck me, we're all tired from working the extreme amount of overtime. It's reasons like this that drive people into a different career field. The captain should have had a conversation with the lieutenant to ensure she understood the operation of the bucket.

As I've already mentioned, this isn't a particularly compelling narrative. It's an eye-opener for people outside corrections to see the type of treatment correctional officers are subject to.

ANONYMOUS QUOTES

The worst job I ever had. The trainers are sexual predators. It's weird because you take an oath and yet so many officers and managers are cheating on spouses or have substance abuse issues. Some went off to prison themselves. Just an awful place to work. You are not working with the sharpest knives in the drawer.

Most toxic place agency I have ever worked for. There is no direction from the executive team, a team with hardly any practical experience.

Management, especially executive management are just a bunch of politicians, they don't really care about you, they have an image to try to convey. The department is extremely soft and good luck getting promoted if you aren't into getting buddy-buddy with management. The department's entire social agenda is a massive joke.

Bad management, people placed into position they are not qualified for. Favoritism, untruest-worthy co-workers and management. Negative environment.

Management has unrealistic expectations for their staff; make staff that excel carry the burden of the workload while those that refuse to do their own duties sluff off; they have no accountability for staff that aren't doing their job.

The good old boy system is set up so if you don't hang out with the right crowd your screwed.

Swat team

Some people must portray themselves as more important than they are. Some individuals consistently engage in this behavior, while others only do so when they are unfamiliar with you and believe they possess significantly more experience than you.

An incident occurred on a unit that involved a significant number of inmates. Following the resolution of the incident, the institution implemented a lockdown, assigning two staff members to each unit. It just so happened that I was assigned the guy who believed he was far more important than he actually was.

I was sitting at the desk, minding my own business, when he entered the unit and introduced himself. I greeted the officer and welcomed him to my unit.

He explained that because of what occurred, he was going to be on my unit for the remainder of the shift. It made no sense to me, as my unit was not involved with the incident, but I'm not in charge, so it is what it is.

About an hour into the shift, I could tell this guy believed I was new by the way he was acting, so I just played along even though my bootlaces had seen more action than him.

He begins by describing his role as a SWAT member and how, prior to his arrival, they were on the verge of retaking the unit. He continued by explaining that their weapons were prepared and ready for action. He described how the inmates surrendered minutes before they entered.

Firstly, I knew we had never lost the unit, so his story was already a fabrication. Second, I knew the man was not on SWAT. Regardless, I just nodded my head and acted like it was cool.

I called up my good friend, who I knew was on SWAT, after he finished bragging about how they were about to tear down the institution and explained the situation to him. My friend was like, Who the fuck does he think he is? He clarified that the man in question is not a member of SWAT and that he has heard of him.

When his trainer, with whom I am also close friends, arrived on the unit, I recounted all the events that had transpired, to which his trainer responded with harsh criticism. He told him even if he was on SWAT, he should not go around talking in case something was

about to go down. I'm not sure how it happened, but the shift lieutenant somehow discovered the conversation and reprimanded him. I don't know where they sent him, but he never returned to the unit, and eventually, for unknown reasons, they let him go.

You can't handle the truth

Every interview seems to include a persistent question that you dread answering. The interviewer asked me to identify one of my shortcomings. Many people don't think of their faults or areas where they can improve before going into an interview. After all, you want the job, so you shouldn't make yourself look bad. You should only highlight your strengths and sell yourself. Make it look as if you're the best candidate for the job. Who has ever landed a job after admitting to being a homicidal maniac, heroin shooter, cocaine snorter, meth addict, or porn addict during an interview? No, you arrive at the interview wearing your best clothes, having brushed your teeth, combed your hair, polished your shoes, and arrived fifteen minutes early. So, when I was asked to name one of my faults, I think I shocked them all when I answered.

With unwavering focus, I addressed the captain. I told him that one of my main faults is truthfulness. I proceeded to explain my approach of being honest and straightforward. After all, all a man has is his word, and if you lie about it, then what good are you?

The captain rubbed his chin for a moment in contemplation before responding. "I would think being truthful would be a beneficial quality, not a fault."

I told him that given enough time, he would understand.

Well, I guess enough time has now passed, and he understands. You see, I've learned from years and years of work that there is always deception, lies, and manipulation from management; sooner or later, he would do the same, and I would call him out on it. In fact, I confronted the entire management team about their recent practice of lying. This, my friends, is why being truthful can be considered a flaw. Had I gone along with their lies, fed into their bullshit, backed them even when we all knew they were wrong, or simply kept my head down and not said shit, I would not be sitting at home. I would be at work right now.

Because management can't handle the truth, their best option was to put me on administrative leave pending an investigation. Have I done anything wrong? Nope. Throughout my tenure, I have never received a written warning or faced any disciplinary action due to oversleeping. I assume that they are currently seeking any evidence they can use against me, as I am still unclear about the purpose of this investigation.

Am I fired as of yet? Nope. Do I think I'm going to lose my job? Absolutely. However, I have gathered sufficient evidence over the past year to pursue a severe lawsuit against the state, although this was not my intended outcome.

The lesson from this story is that if you're not prepared to fight, simply remain silent when management confronts you with their falsehoods.

YOU CAN'T HANDLE THE TRUTH

Suicide watch

It doesn't matter whether you are an officer, corporal, sergeant, lieutenant, or captain. There are policies and procedures in the world of corrections that you must adhere to. No one is exempt, regardless of how important you think you are. One captain disregarded the rules, policies, and procedures, acting according to his own desires.

It seems he volunteered for a suicide watch. Great, I know of nobody who likes to do a suicide watch. The process is painful. You sit in the uncomfortable chair, barely more comfortable than a bag of nails, and continuously observe the inmate through the small window. It's eight hours of pure hell. Whether the inmate is pacing, sleeping, jacking his junk, cussing, swearing, or playing in his shit, you are required to sit and document everything.

The rules of segregation still apply. You do not have the door open unless there is another staff member with you. Let me repeat that. You should never open the door without the presence of another staff member. Even if the inmate starts to do self-harm, you pepper spray him through the food flap and wait for more staff to arrive.

As the day passed, an officer who was working his unit was relieved from his post and instructed to relieve the captain and assume responsibility for the suicide watch. No harm, no foul. That's the reality of being a flex. Sometimes you're the bug, and sometimes you're the windshield. When the officer arrived at segregation to relieve the captain, the captain had the door open, sitting inside the cell with the inmate's feet kicked up, drinking coffee, and relaxing.

This must rank among the most significant infractions in the history of corrections. Why didn't the other officers in segregation speak up or take any action? If a captain had caught me in that situation, they would have immediately walked me out. It was a grave breach of the corrections policy.

Not sleeping

There's no denying the possibility of occasionally dozing off during the graveyard shift. Most of the time, this happens inadvertently, but there are instances where it is intentional. This just so happens to be the case where someone was not sleeping on shift and got accused of it and sent home.

I know this story to be factual because I was on the phone with them when it happened.

The sergeant walked onto the unit and blatantly accused the officer of sleeping.

The officer defended themselves, saying that they were not sleeping but on the phone.

The sergeant remained resolute, insisting that he had caught them sleeping. I'm not sure what his intentions were; perhaps he wanted to establish a reputation with management to increase his chances of promotion.

The officer was still on the phone with me at this point, and I could hear him defending the fact that they weren't sleeping.

The sergeant was hearing none of it and went and reported it to the shift lieutenant that they caught officer _____ sleeping.

Without question, the shift lieutenant sent the officer home because he believed they were unfit for duty.

When I took my break, I went straight to the lieutenant and called bullshit, as I know for a fact that they were not sleeping as I was talking with them on the phone. I heard the entire conversation and repeated it to the lieutenant.

The lieutenant offered justifications, stating that they likely contacted me following their apprehension.

Again, I called bullshit, as I was the one that called them, and we had been talking for a good fifteen minutes, if not longer, before the sergeant showed up.

The lieutenant was having none of it and congratulated the sergeant on a job well done.

Sleeping

Like most things in life, honesty, even when it's difficult, is the best policy in the long run. This statement would have held true in the next story and possibly saved his job.

The officer was sound asleep on the unit.

The lieutenant was making the rounds and did not try to be quiet or sneak up on the officer; he was simply doing his job. He called for the unit door, walked towards the officer's station, and noticed the officer sleeping. He then took out his state-provided cell phone and recorded the officer sleeping for at least five minutes before waking him.

At that moment, he awakened the officer, who denied having been asleep. (Smart move, stupid.) Instead of just admitting he was sleeping and saying he fucked up, he continued to argue with the lieutenant.

At this point, the lieutenant decided to send the officer home. He called for me to come to the unit immediately, which I complied with.

Upon my arrival, I witnessed a heated argument between the officer and the lieutenant. I stood there waiting for a good five minutes trying to decipher what in the hell was actually going on. The lieutenant then explained to me that I would be taking over the unit.

I asked how long I was going to be there, and the lieutenant said the rest of the night.

On the way out, the officer mumbled something I couldn't understand, which further agitated the lieutenant. I observed the pair walking across the compound through the door's window.

After that I never saw the officer again. During the investigation into the incident, I learned that the officer persisted in lying, claiming he wasn't sleeping, until the lieutenant played a video from his phone, which proved he was. I can only surmise that ethics violations led to the officer's termination. Had he just told the truth, he would still be working there today.

Tampering with evidence

As much as I would hate to think that management would intentionally screw me over, there is no other logical conclusion that I can come to.

There was a fight on a different unit that must have been a decent brawl, as the responding staff said that they were going to need hazmat to come to the unit with the blood spill kit.

The hazmat inmate is currently residing on my unit, and I was anticipating a call instructing me to send him to the unit where the fight occurred.

What actually happened, though, was completely unexplainable, beyond the fact that the officer who entered my unit was looking to instigate something.

The officer entered my unit and walked straight towards the officer's station. The officer shoved me aside, took hold of the unit phone, and summoned the hazmat inmate to the officer's station. After they departed the officer's station, they met the inmate halfway down the tier.

I informed the officer that they could have just called me and told me to send the inmate.

The officer responded with, "Well, I was already here."

No, you were not already here. You entered my unit solely to cause trouble.

When I got relieved, I went directly to the lieutenant and demanded a copy of the video, as I had just been technically assaulted by another staff member. I gave him the exact location and the time. The lieutenant is aware that DOC rules require an investigation into all assaults.

The lieutenant informed me that the captain would need to authorize him to burn the video. I asked him to call the captain, and the lieutenant said no. He instructed me to send an email to the captain, which I did, but I never received a response or any further updates on the incident. What better way to tamper with evidence than to let it get recorded over?

I never said that

One would think that as much as management preaches ethics, they would follow what they preach. This assumption couldn't be more inaccurate. When confronted, management consistently responds with the same response: "I never said that."

Having dealt with the bullshit long enough, I had a meeting with the captain where I explained everything I was experiencing from a select group of employees. He advised me to avoid working near them until the situation was rectified.

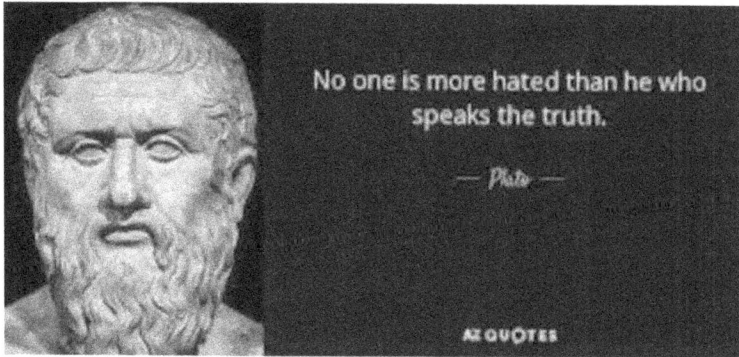

No one is more hated than he who speaks the truth.

— Plato —

AZ QUOTES

As time passed, the onslaught of attacks continued even though I made every effort to avoid the offending party while still doing my job with professionalism. I eventually met with HR to discuss the unwarranted attacks, and as expecting, it went nowhere. What I didn't expect was the way she covered for management to the point of gaslighting me.

Instead of looking into the situation as she should have, the HR woman went directly to the captain and relayed everything we discussed which was a breach of confidentiality. I didn't care though because everything I stated was the truth. However, this put me at odds with the captain, and he turned against me.

The next meeting was to be with the captain's superior, but he demanded that the captain be present. During this meeting when I was asking about the current investigation, the captain interrupted me and became irate and yelled, "I never told you that you cannot work with them."

That is a bold-faced, lying-through-your-filthy-teeth statement. The captain did in fact say that. What's even worse is the fact that another captain witnessed him saying this, yet that captain refused to step up and tell him that he did indeed make that statement.

If I had been lying in such a drastic manner, I would have been walked out. Well, I did the only thing I could do, and that was to file a formal complaint, which landed me in even more hot water. I suppose it's accurate to say that management expects the truth, except when it pertains to themselves.

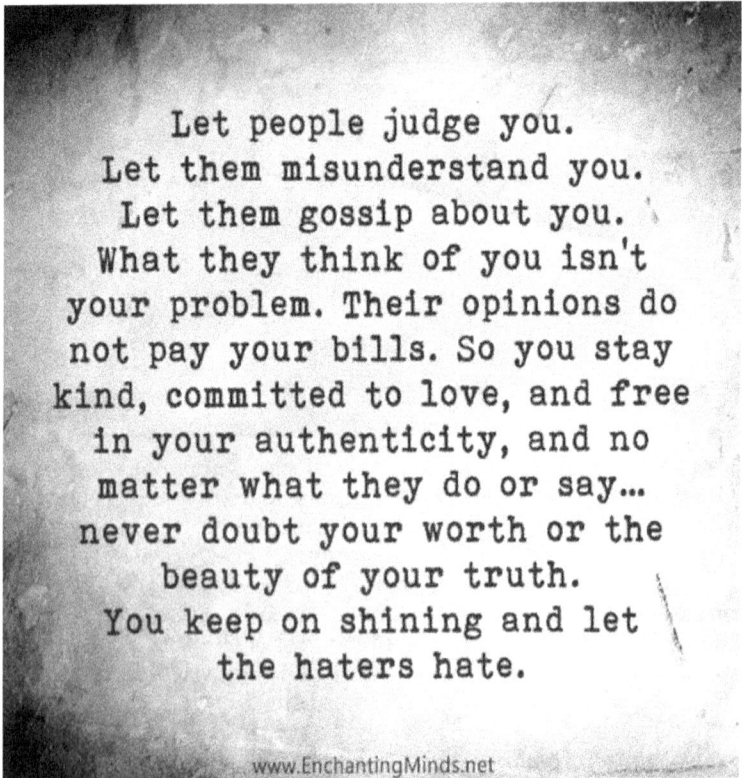

Let people judge you.
Let them misunderstand you.
Let them gossip about you.
What they think of you isn't
your problem. Their opinions do
not pay your bills. So you stay
kind, committed to love, and free
in your authenticity, and no
matter what they do or say...
never doubt your worth or the
beauty of your truth.
You keep on shining and let
the haters hate.

www.EnchantingMinds.net

Shots fired

Not all lies come from management; some come directly from the correctional officers. This is dangerous because many officers believe they are telling the truth as they spew lies.

This is the story of a fight that occurred on the yard. What started with two inmates turned into an all-out brawl. Lacking the staff to quell the disturbance, one inmate seized the opportunity to stomp on another inmate's head in a blatant attempt to murder the unconscious inmate.

The tower officer acted within the parameters of his post and intervened before the inmate killed the unconscious inmate. The officer fired a single shot, killing the inmate instantly. Had he not intervened, the inmate would have most certainly died.

THE MOST DANGEROUS LIARS ARE THOSE WHO THINK THEY ARE TELLING THE TRUTH

All the inmates got down as instructed, and the institution went into lockdown. When an inmate dies in such a manner, the institution follows standard operating procedures.

Enter the lie.

Unaware of my presence that day, the officer initiated a conversation with some other staff. The officer started discussing the shooting incident, emphasizing that they were the only ones who intervened after the inmate's shooting. This officer persisted in her fabrication, insisting that the institution should halt operations in the yard until she had cleaned up the large blood puddle.

Again, after the shooting, the narcissist saw a perfect opportunity to validate their presence and rewrite the story so that they emerge as the hero.

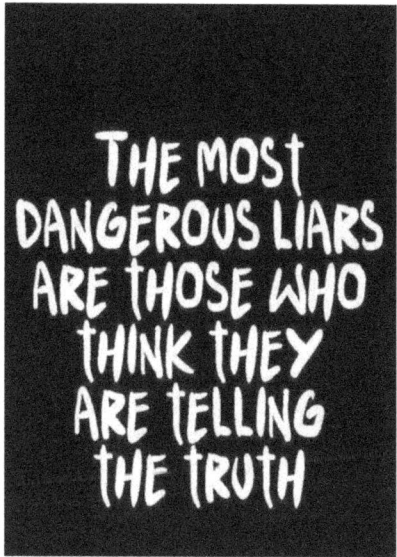

Any individual possessing a modicum of common sense understands that an institution enters a state of lockdown upon the shooting and death of an inmate. I find it astounding that they would believe otherwise.

Bonus Tale

A friend of mine whom I have come to know by the book, Betty, is a stickler for the rules. Apparently, one night, she entered her unit and became extremely upset upon witnessing inmates occupying the dayroom. Wondering what the hell was going on, she stormed into the officer's station searching for an answer.

The inmates appear to have received permission to leave their cells in order to polish and wax the floor. She refused to comply, as she believed it was not appropriate.

She experienced what many would consider a breakdown. What she truly needed was to discover Jesus Christ. Well, she called the lieutenant and lost her shit on him about how management just does whatever the fuck they want to around this place and how nobody gives a fuck. She was yelling and screaming at the inmates, kicking shit over, and throwing chairs.

The sergeant called me up and asked if I could get her under control before they send her home. I agreed to try and dial the number. I was looking out the window at her unit, and just then, to my surprise, a mop bucket sailed across the dayroom.

I couldn't decide whether to engage in conversation with her or burst into laughter. When she answered the phone, she was still screaming and yelling and throwing shit out into the dayroom. I'm not sure how I managed to calm her down to the point where she wasn't sent home, but they never again attempted to wax the floor when the inmates knew she would be on post.

Inmates and comedy

Behind the cold stone walls and concertina topped chain link fences, inmates are faced with many perils. They are always at the risk of assault, gang pressure, retaliation from other inmates, the constant risk of getting written up, shanked, celled in, or sent to the hole. Through all this you can still find the occasional inmate who's gifted with an uncanny sense of humor. Not just any sense of humor, but the special kind that would keep two angry men from fighting and leave them bent over laughing with tears in their eyes and then they would walk away as friends. I've had the chance to encounter a few inmates like this and always kept what they said locked away in a folder in the back of my mind to use at a later date. I believe the time has come now to open the doors and allow these incidents to flow fourth onto the pages so we all can enjoy the laughter.

Mop bucket

What we have here is a combination of sheer stupidity, and utter brilliance. The time was early morning, and the Inmate orderlies were just waking up and getting prepared for cell sanitation. I sat at the desk patiently watching them get the mops ready, put on a new duster for the dust mop, organize the brooms and dust pans in an orderly fashion, all while talking shit to each other how none of them knew their jobs properly.

Occasionally, I would chuckle as one inmate burned the others in a true fashion of disrespect. Thinking we were just about to be ready to begin this highly detailed and extremely organized operation with surgeon like precision, an inmate neared the desk and asked if I had a black marker.

"Why," I asked.

"We got a new mop bucket yesterday and I need to write on it what it's for."

"Ah, okay," I mumbled, then proceeded to hand him a permanent black sharpie.

The inmate snatched the sharpie as if it was a gift from god and proceeded to write, "Tears only."

I damn near buck snorted, then blew snot across the desk as I gripped my side laughing.

"What?" the inmate asked.

"You spelled tears as if someone is crying. You should have spelled it as T.I.E.R.S., which means a hallway," all the while still laughing.

"Ah shit," the inmate said as he determined the best way to fix his fuck up. Deciding there was no right way to correct the spelling, he handed the marker back and said, "Ah fuck it, they can't read anyways."

HURT FEELINGS REPORT

DATE: _____

TIME OF HURTFULNESS: _____ AM/PM

A. Which ear were words of hurtfulness spoken into: LEFT / RIGHT / BOTH
B. Is there permanent feeling damage: YES / NO
C. Did you require a tissue for the tears: YES / NO

Reasons for filing this report. (Check Box)

1. I am thin skinned ☐
2. I am a pussy ☐
3. I have woman like hormones ☐
4. I am a queer ☐
5. I am a little bitch ☐
6. I am a cry baby ☐
7. I want my mommy ☐
8. My butt is easliy hurt ☐
9. All of the above ☐

Name of "Real Man" who hurt your sensitive little feelings: _____

We, as a company, take hurt feelings very seriously. If you don't have a mommy that can give you a hug and make it all better, please let your supervisor know and we can provide you with a surrogate. If you need them, diapers, midol and a "blanky" can also be supplied.

Name little sissy filing report: _____

Girly-man signature: _____

Real-man signature: _____
(person being accused)

Supervisor:

_____

Phone call

There's a time in every person's life when you hear something that just shocks you to the core. My time came about nine in the morning as I sat at the officer's desk. Just to the left of the officer's desk was a bank of phones. Each one sat empty except for one, where an inmate spoke to his wife. Nothing out of the ordinary, nor unusual.

All that changed when the conversation went from her and what she was doing to talking about her boyfriend. They discussed where he was working, the vehicle he recently purchased, what she was cooking for dinner, how the kids were doing, and so much more. I know I shouldn't have done it, but it was like a bad train wreck. I just couldn't look away or stop listening.

When the conversation ended, he hung up the phone and started to walk back to his bunk. I called him over to the officer's station, where he promptly came.

"What's up, Harris?" he asked.

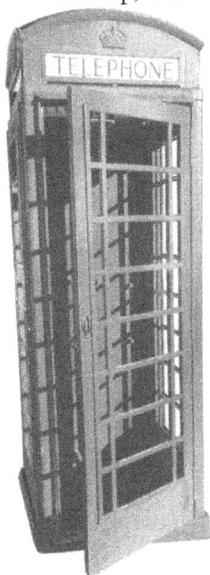

I thought for a minute before I spoke. "Now I know this is none of my business," I calmly explained. "I just happen to hear your phone conversation."

"Yes, so," he said.

I cautiously continued. "For a time, you talked with your wife, but then it turned to her boyfriend. You don't have a problem with her having a boyfriend?"

The inmate never missed a beat, never hesitated, never turned away in shame, nor did he get pissed. He looked me dead in the face and said, "I don't care who's she's fucking as long as he gets out when I get out."

I stood there blinking, unsure what to say.

The inmate waited patiently, as he knew I was about to pass out from what I heard.

Gathering my composure, I finally

spoke. "What happens if he doesn't want to get out? What happens if he likes it there? A lot can change between now and when you're released."

The inmate had an answer for that as well. "If he doesn't want to get out, then I will."

"Okay," I said. "Sounds like a plan."

I watched the inmate walk back to his bunk. To this day, I have yet to hear another phone call from an inmate who is happy that his wife is getting plowed by another man while he's locked up.

LMFAO

A man had a 25" long penis and it created difficulties in his life as it was not easy to move around with it and women were afraid of him too. He also had a very high pitched voice.

He went to see a doctor. "What can I do about my enormous penis?" he asked in a high pitched voice.

The doctor examined him carefully. "Your penis is so large that you can't get any blood to your vocal chords. But we can do a penis transplant, to give you a normal sized penis, and that will fix your voice."

The man thought about it. "Okay," he said in his high pitched voice.

He woke up after the operation and he felt great. His new penis was a normal size. He could walk, he could run, and best of all, his voice was completely normal!

But after a few weeks he realized having a 25-inch penis was pretty cool. Finally he went back to the doctor. "I've thought about it and I would like to undo the operation."

"That's impossible," the doctor said in a high pitched voice.

Is that chocolate

I don't believe there has ever been a time in my life when I felt so disgusted. I was sitting at the officer's desk doing my thing; the unit was basically running itself. The section where the inmates undress for the showers is located just to my right. It's a small space, just big enough to accommodate one inmate. They have a large white flap in place, akin to a swinging door, to conceal their junk from observation.

On this day the inmate thought it would be enjoyable to play a game. As I went about my usual business, he called out to me.

"What do you need?" I yelled from the desk and looked in his

direction.

The inmate held up his underwear and showed me the crotch area. There was a streak mark that extended from one end to the other. I have not seen a skid mark like that since my kids were in diapers. "My God," I said. "Did you shit your drawers?"

The inmate started laughing. However, his subsequent actions deeply disturbed me. It drove a stake of disgust right down into my soul. How I held back the lump of vomit that gathered in my throat is still beyond me.

The inmate began to lick the shit by holding the underwear up to his mouth.

I came up out of my chair like a ballistic missile. "Are you fucking serious?" I screamed.

The inmate laughed even harder as he licked it again.

I wasn't sure if I should confront the inmate or just walk away and pretend that nothing had happened.

After the inmate stopped laughing, he informed me it was actually melted chocolate, and he was just messing around.

I investigated the poo with a good sniff to verify, then looked at the inmate and said, "These underwear is still dirty, you freak."

He said, "Nah, they're clean. I just got them today."

I responded with. "It doesn't matter. A few days ago, another inmate had those on his ass and sweaty balls.

The inmate didn't care. He simply laughed once more before entering the shower.

Spider man

Working in corrections I have done thousands of searches. Most of the time, these searches are mundane and boring. You hope to uncover a hidden stash of drugs, tattoo paraphernalia, a weapon, a sharpened toothbrush, and a disassembled razor. Most of the time, however, your role resembles that of a maid. You take away a bunch of garbage, nuisance contraband that doesn't mean shit. OHHH, look at me, I found two extra pairs of socks… Whoop de fucking do? Get the newspaper on the phone.

This search, on the other hand, was the most unusual of its kind. I opened up his storage box and began rummaging through the mass pile of shit. How he could find anything in the shithole was beyond me. Why did I even choose this inmate? Perhaps it was a cruel joke from God that influenced my decision. Nearing the search's completion, I found a clamshell styrofoam container near the bottom.

I had already gathered half a bag of garbage, so what is one more item? Mumbling something along the lines of, "What a fucking pig," I grab the container, expecting it to be light, but it had a bit of weight to it. Believing I had finally discovered something noteworthy, such as a tattoo motor, I began to open the styrofoam container to examine the contents.

Holy Lord Jesus Christ. Two long, hairy legs shot outwards in an attempt to grab me.

I dropped the goddamn thing as if it were on fire. It lands on the heap of debris in his box and flips open. To my astonishment and horror, the largest spider I've ever seen darts toward me. This thing resembled a disgruntled Volkswagen Beetle approaching me.

I screamed so loudly, like a little bitch, that it hurt my ears, and then I ran halfway across the unit, fully aware that this fucker was on my tracks, ready to devour me.

When I looked back, the inmates were laughing hysterically.

"What the fuck is that thing?" I yelled.

"It's my pet," the inmate said.

"Get that fucking thing and get it outside," I told the inmate. "How do you know it's not poisonous? It could be sick or something."

The inmate explained it's just a common tarantula and not poisonous. He continues with, "I found this one right outside the unit by the door. I've had him for a few weeks now."

I am uncertain as to what the inmate was feeding this eight-legged death machine; however, its excessive weight suggests that it was consuming a sumptuous diet. Then it hit me. A few officers had not been seen in a while, and I wondered if they were the latest victims.

With disappointment in his eyes, he collected the spider and took it outside; they said their goodbyes and then parted ways.

NOT A GODDAMN PET

What's for breakfast

It was a dark and stormy night… Not really; I just always wanted to begin a story that way. It was night, though, and an eerie silence drifted over the unit. The bathrooms were empty, and the only sound I could hear was the whisper from the computer. I settled in expecting a mundane shift when the silence was broken by an inmate who began talking in his sleep.

This is not an uncommon occurrence, as inmates often engage in such activities. Hell, I've probably done it but don't remember.

However, the inmate's constant tone changes led to a heated conversation—with himself, of course. After about twenty minutes, an inmate approached the desk and asked if I could help him stop waking others up with his self-centered dispute.

I agreed that things were starting to spiral out of control, so I went to his bunk and gently tapped on his bed with my flashlight.

"What, what, what?" The inmate said as he sat up, baffled as to why I was standing there.

"You're talking and arguing with yourself in your sleep," I told him. "You're starting to wake others up."

"I'm sorry, C/O," he apologized.

"Don't worry about it," I said, then started heading back to the officers station. Before I reached the desk, the inmate must have fallen back asleep and said, "Now look what you've done," in a completely different tone. I could not help but start laughing. He did stay quiet the rest of the night.

-Fast forward to morning-

I switch on the lights, and the unit begins to awaken. The inmate, who had been arguing with himself, decided to check the breakfast menu. What transpired next is undoubtedly the most bizarre event I have ever witnessed.

The inmate is standing at the board and asks himself if he wants pancakes. In a completely different tone, he says that he is not in the mood for pancakes. In a third tone, he asserts that pancakes aren't all that bad.

He then reverts back to the original voice and says that pancakes sound good. No, they do not; the other voice comes back. "What's wrong with pancakes?" he asks himself.

This inmate is arguing with himself in three distinct voices about whether he wants pancakes for breakfast.

Finally, I have no choice but to intervene, telling him that he needs to make a decision and return to his bunk.

My unit eventually gets called for breakfast, and I watch him leave. Around thirty minutes later he returns, and I ask him if he had pancakes. He replies that he had one, so I replied, I guess one of your personalities ate.

He just shook his head and mumbled something, then walked back to his bunk.

Two young brothers are up in their room. The older of the brothers says to the younger, "I think it's time we start cussing."

The younger brother agrees. "But what do we say?" he asks.

The older brother thinks for a moment, then says, "At breakfast, I'll say hell and you say damn."

"Okay," the younger brother agrees.

Eventually their mother calls them down for breakfast.

Once they arrive their mother asks the older of the two what he wants for breakfast. "Ah, hell, give me cheerios," he says.

The woman rips him from his chair, spanks his ass, then sends him back to his room. Next she turns to the younger brother and asks him the same thing.

The younger boy says, "I damn sure don't want Cheerios."

The bean flicker

We've all participated in horseplay, even though it's not the best behavior to practice. We've all engaged in activities such as wrestling around and sticking our wet fingers in the other person's ear. This time, the situation escalated between the inmates, leading to serious consequences for one of them.

It was lunchtime, and the workers were still eating their meal before the units were called down. Well, one inmate saw his friend across the chow hall and decided now was the perfect time to strike.

It just so happened that they were having pinto beans as a side with their lunch. What better ammo to strike your buddy with than a nice, good, solid bean that fits perfectly in the inmate's plastic spoon?

He loaded the weapon, bent the spoon back until it was almost ready to snap, aimed at his target, and then fired.

The bean shot out like a rocket, damn near breaking the sound barrier.

The inmates who still ate were completely unaware of the missile that sailed a mere foot over their heads.

The bean, being non-aerodynamic, began to turn about halfway to the target, as if it were guided by some ultra-high electronic computer, and went straight for the officer who was standing across the room.

The bean struck the officer's neck with an impact equivalent to that of a Mack truck. Jello-like waves of fat rolled up and down the officer's neck.

The officer let out a scream, as if a thousand dead pimps had just slapped them.

"What the fuck" they screamed, holding their neck,

To my surprise, the inmate confessed to everything, claiming he was attempting to harm his friend. The inmate was restrained and taken to segregation. Initially, they planned to charge the inmate with officer assault, but ultimately, they reduced it to mere horseplay.

Indentation

There are things that happen during cell searches that are purely accidental. You may drop their coffee and spill it on the floor, accidentally bend a drawing, or confiscate something unintended. Some incidents, like the following, seem intentional and cannot be considered accidents.

It began with a typical cell search. The inmate was moved to the dayroom as they are not permitted to watch during the search. During the search, the officer found the typical contraband: empty containers, garbage, an altered pen, and the usual items we always seem to find.

It was not until the search was concluded that anything out of the ordinary was discovered. As the inmate reorganized his belongings in his drawer, he noticed a partially unscrewed lid on his peanut butter. As he unscrewed the lid, something unexpected happened. Located in the brand new jar of peanut butter was the indentation of a penis, as if the searcher had slapped his junk against the smooth surface.

The inmate expressed a desire to speak with the sergeant immediately, followed by the lieutenant. The inmate filed a grievance and demanded a new jar of peanut butter.

I'm not sure if the inmate was lying, but it appears to be an unusual attempt to obtain a new jar of peanut butter. Regarding the officer, I am uncertain if he received any reprimand for this action, given that it was the inmate's word against the staff. In my mind, they should have had the officer drop his drawers and match them up with the mushroom indent.

Regardless, I have never looked at a jar of peanut butter the same way. Regarding the inmate, I suspect he received a fresh jar of peanut butter, but I cannot confirm this with certainty.

Shocking

Just when you thought an inmate couldn't get any stupider, they do something even dumber. For some inexplicable reason, the inmate believed he could build up a resistance by repeatedly shocking himself in his cell at night. I'm uncertain whether he read an article, heard this from another prisoner, or independently came up with this theory.

Regardless of where he obtained this information, he was unaware that building up a tolerance to electricity is not possible, unlike building up a tolerance to substances like drugs or alcohol. He forgot that the human nervous system and our heart communicate with electrochemical signals. It doesn't take a lightning bolt to kill you.

Anyway, after months of shocking himself in his cell, he decided to make the move at sunset and made a mad dash for the perimeter fence. The first fence is easy, as it's just a regular chain-link fence. The concertina wire slowed him down a bit, but the second fence is where he met his fate.

The large glowing sign indicating "Danger: High Voltage" held no significance. After all, he had been preparing for this for months.

Without hesitation he leaped for the fence. Freedom was just on the other side.

No more having to ask to take a shit. He would no longer have to endure long lines for unappealing food at the chow hall. In a few days he'd be back in town getting some pussy. Even the air smelled different this close to the fence. There was a freshness you couldn't quite find on the unit. The rancid smell of B.O. and urine permeated the unit. The place reeked of depression. Yes, freedom was only a twenty-foot climb.

The inmate struck the fence with the intention of crossing it in a matter of seconds. Instead, the tower reported a large blue flash and a loud popping, crackling sound, reminiscent of a fly hitting a bug zapper. Control sent a mobile in that direction, thinking it might be a coyote, but the scene revealed something else. An inmate lay just inside of the fence, dead. The inmate's clothing was still smoking from the internal burns beneath it. Another Darwin Award was successfully handed out.

How to make money

A small kid asked his wealthy self-made friend (that is also a small kid) the secret behind him making hundreds of dollars every time he speaks to an adult that he knows, and his buddy replied "the secret is telling the adult I know everything, they will simply tell you to keep your mouth shut and hand you a ton of money". So the little kid went home to his mother and said "mom, I know everything!" So his mother told him to shut up and not tell anyone, and handed him a thousand dollars. The kid then tried the same thing with his dad, and his dad told him to keep his mouth shut and not tell anyone, and handed him 2 thousand dollars. The kid got excited and went outside to try it on other adults he knew in the neighborhood. First person he sees is the mailman, the kid says "Hello Mr. Mailman! I know everything!" Then the mail man said "REALLY?? COME GIVE DADDY A HUG!!"

The sword

Warning: Not all inmate stories are funny. Sometimes, they can be downright scary.

This story begins in the most unlikely of places, out in the yard. The inmate worked on a crew that was designated to walk around with wheelbarrows and collect any rocks that were considered large enough to cause serious harm or death. Once the wheelbarrow was considered full, the inmate would transport the filled wheelbarrow to a central area. At night, during the institution's lockdown, maintenance would arrive with a bucket loader and remove them.

This particular day was extremely hot. Exhausted, the inmate rested on the wheelbarrow's edge. The officer, being the dick that he was, kicked the wheelbarrow over, spilling the rocks and causing the inmate to fall onto his ass. The officer yelled and screamed at him to pick up the rocks and get his ass moving.

They say an elephant never forgets; well, neither does an inmate.

Fast forward a bit, and the inmate secured a new job in the metal shop. In his spare time, and without anyone knowing, he slowly worked a flat piece of steel into a sword that was nearly three feet long.

This was not just a simple slab of metal. It boasted a graceful curve, a sharpened edge capable of effortlessly slicing through flesh and bone, a beautifully wrapped wooden handle, and was nearly ready for use.

Fortunately, an inmate working in the metal shop informed the staff about the weapon's well-hidden location. That particular inmate wanted no part of this, as he liked his job in the metal shop.

Uncertain about who made the weapon, they took it but secretly watched to see who went where it had been hidden.

Upon discovery, they cuffed and escorted the inmate to segregation, where they questioned him. Come to find out, it was the same inmate who was kicked off the wheelbarrow that day in the yard, and he spoke with complete seriousness when he admitted that he planned to behead the officer right in the yard where everyone could see.

Most likely, an officer would have shot him right away, but the inmate didn't care. He 100% planned to kill that officer and any officer who got in his way. The institution immediately made an emergency transfer of the inmate to an undisclosed institution.

SNAILCALIBUR THE GREAT

Damn key

In all my years of working in corrections, there is one thing I've learned. Expect the unexpected. This was the one instance where I did not anticipate the unexpected, and it stung me deeply.

I was in the officer's station, which sits in the middle of the unit. An inmate comes up to the window and asks if he can talk to me alone for a minute.

"Sure," I say, and depart the officer's station.

After leaving the officer's station and closing the door, I realized I had forgotten the radio, as we had no other means to carry it except in our cargo pocket or in your hand. The officer's station door automatically locks when you close it.

I instruct the inmate to hold on for a moment while they try to unlock the door, but the damn key snaps. *You Can't Make This Shit Up.*

Well, shit. What do I do now? I don't have a radio to call control to send over key control to bring me a new key. I don't have a phone, as the phones are corded and attached to the desk. As a last resort, I dispatch an inmate to the adjacent unit to instruct the officer to send a sergeant who I know has a spare key.

The inmate panics. He rushes to the next unit and informs the officer that he doesn't understand what's happening, but the officer on the other unit urgently needs assistance.

The officer in that unit panics and I assume calls out on the radio something along the lines of that I am being killed on the unit.

As I lean against the door, waiting for the sergeant, half the institution bursts through, ready to go. I was surrounded by officers, sergeants, lieutenants, counselors, caseworkers, cooks, and maintenance staff, all of whom were curious about what was happening.

Holy shit, were they all pissed that all this commotion was caused by a broken key.

Police & Thieves cocktail

2 oz gin

0.5 oz cinnamon simple syrup,

0.5 oz pineapple juice

0.5 oz fresh lime juice

.25 oz fresh grapefruit juice

Ꜧave a drink on me

There is one undeniable fact when it comes to correctional officers, alcohol is a big part of how they unwind after work. The problem is, is that one drink turns into two, two to three, three to four until the officer becomes an alcoholic.

According to one study, it is shown that 70.8% used alcohol in the last month. This same study also showed that there is a direct link between alcohol use and officer burnout. Other studies have found that correctional officers drink more than the general population. Mental health issues, such as PTSD, are common among correctional officers, and are directly linked to substance abuse. Correctional officers often lack access to stress management resources and healthy coping mechanisms. More than half of correctional officers say they wouldn't ask their employer for help with stress, and nearly a third wouldn't ask for help with substance use.

Risky sexual behaviors have been correlated with alcohol use in multiple studies. This is partly due to alcohol's negative effect on a person's ability to think, plan, and reasonably evaluate situations, potentially leading to increased sexual risk taking.

Most correctional officers deal with chronic high stress, long tumultuous shifts, and a constant requirement for high-level anxiety based on the nature of the job. Because of this they turn to alcohol to find relief. The stories told in this next section are all alcohol related and none of them end well.

LOL

A man walks into a bar and sees his friend sitting beside a 12-inch pianist. He says to his friend, "That's amazing. Where did he come from?"

The friend pulls out an old lamp and tells him the genie inside will grant him one wish. The man rubs the bottle, and to his amazement, a puff of purple smoke spews out and slowly collects in the form of a genie. In a booming voice, the genie tells the man he has but one wish.

The man thinks and says, "I wish I had a million bucks." Suddenly, the bar is filled with ducks, bursting from the door and windows, standing on top of the bar, dunking their heads into people's drinks. "What just happened?!" the guy asks.

His friend replies, "I know. Did you really think I wanted a twelve-inch pianist?"

The phone

NOTE: Although I was not present during the incident, I heard about it from a third party and confirmed the veracity of the story with the person it happened to.

Alcohol changes your way of thinking. The more alcohol you consume, the more foolish you become. When they drink, some people become angry and want to fight everyone, while others turn into Casanovas, believing they are the perfect match for any woman. There is no steadfast rule, though, of what people will do. This is a story of a weekend camping trip out with the coworkers that went terribly wrong.

It was a planned weekend camping trip with the coworkers. Once in the mountains, the first thing to emerge after setting up the tents is the refreshing ice-cold beer. As the sun sinks low in the western sky and darkness falls across the land, a fire usually starts. Usually, people gather around the fire to enjoy the warmth and start sharing their stories.

As the night continues and the beer cans accumulate, the stories deepen, inspiring people to take risks they might not have otherwise taken. It's always inevitable that someone will pass out first, and it's never the person you expect.

When you start drinking, you don't want to pass out first. No good ever comes from that. Typically, you awaken with a hotdog sticking in your mouth and a dick drawn on your forehead. You are never certain of the pranks that others will devise to embarrass you at a later time.

What they devised this time was the most heinous scheme I have ever encountered in all my years of alcohol consumption. They stole the officer's phone, called his wife, and assumed his identity. It gets worse. Once they had the officer's wife on the phone, they attempted to persuade her to send some nude selfies.

Fortunately, she suspected that this was not her husband, as he would never inquire about it. Therefore, she sent a few pictures of herself in a bikini. She made a wise decision, but who can predict what would have happened if she had sent nude images?

When questioned about their behavior, the officer who concocted the scheme said that he was only joking. I call bullshit. You don't ask someone else's wife to send nude pictures, then claim that you're just joking. This must be the most heinous act you could possibly commit against your so-called friend.

The bracelets

In the world of corrections, where ethics and honorable behavior mean everything, it's rough to recover from a DWI (driving while intoxicated). If you receive two DWIs, your job may be in jeopardy. If you get three DWIs, holy shit, how is that even possible? What's even worse than receiving three DWIs is having to wear an ankle bracelet, which allows law enforcement to track your location and ensure you stay away from bars.

I KNEW A GUY WHO WAS PLACED ON HOUSE ARREST. PROBLEM IS, THE ANKLE MONITOR WAS PLACED ON HIS ARTIFICIAL LEG, SO HE STILL LEFT THE HOUSE WHENEVER HE WANTED, HE JUST LEFT A LEG BEHIND.

I don't judge, so nothing this officer does bothers me. He can drink and drive as much as he wants as long as I am not involved in the accident.

What concerns me is how he maintained his job, given that I have witnessed individuals with significantly fewer infractions being dismissed. However, I realized that the officer's close friendship with the management and frequent golf outings could potentially qualify this situation as nepotism. The officer's most recent DWI involved him driving through a fence and then colliding with a barn. Please explain to me exactly how this officer was not let go. I can articulate the rationale, which stems from the management's close relationship. To this day I am still not even sure if it is legal for the officer to wear an ankle bracelet inside the institution.

To continue with the story, the officer came onto my unit at count time. Upon his arrival, I expressed my confusion about the situation. He asked me what the problem was.

I asked if I was supposed to count him as well, and he just laughed and said, "Nope, they counted me in county."

One might assume that having three DWIs on your record would negatively impact your potential for promotion. Nope, the officer has moved up through the ranks… Go figure. My record is impeccable, but I was told I would never go anywhere because I am not part of the system. Go figure once more.

Today at the bank, an old lady asked me to help check her balance. So I pushed her over.

What pole

The night was like any other night. As I sat in the darkness, with minimal radio activity, a faint melody drifted through the speakers. I had AC/DC playing on the computer with the song "You Shook Me All Night Long." I had already finished all my required duties, so now it was time to relax and let the night pass.

About three hours into the shift, I heard a disturbing call on the radio. Uh... long pause. Uh... long pause... Uh... long pause.

I recognized my friend's voice, but I was uncertain about his intended message. I knew it wasn't a fight between inmates, or an inmate hanging up, or something stupid because he was working the mobile. It was something, though, and it had him quite concerned.

The next radio call confirmed that something was amiss, as my buddy requested the shift lieutenant to meet him out front.

I went to the window and started scanning the area but couldn't see anything. I would have no choice but to wait and talk to him personally to find out what happened.

An hour or so later I noticed flashing yellow lights on the road that circles the institution. Shortly after, a tow truck came by, hauling away one of the mobiles. The damn thing must have broken down, I assumed, knowing how the state maintains their vehicles.

That morning I ran into my buddy and asked him what the hell happened.

He shook his head in disbelief as he started to explain. "Well, I was following the other mobile around the institution when the vehicle in front of me suddenly swerved left, then right, then left, and finally swerved right into a pole." The impact was so intense that one of the front tires folded up beneath the vehicle.

I got out and went to the vehicle, making sure the

officer was alright, then called for the lieutenant to meet me up front.

After taking the officer to the hospital, authorities discovered he was highly intoxicated. The alarming aspect of this situation is that the officer drove to work while intoxicated, drove a state vehicle while intoxicated, and then crashed a state vehicle while intoxicated.

The institution conducted its own investigation into the accident instead of calling the state police. The investigation's outcome involved removing him from his position and placing him in a housing unit. Fortunately, the incident did not result in any injuries or fatalities.

A priest and a rabbi are in a car crash and it's pretty bad.

Both of their cars are totaled but neither one of them is hurt.

After they crawl out of their cars, the rabbi says, "So you're a priest. That's interesting; I'm a rabbi. Wow, just look at our cars! There's nothing left to either one of them but we're unhurt. This must be a sign from God that we should meet and be friends and live together in peace."

The priest replies, "Oh, yes, I agree. It's a miracle that we survived and are here together."

"And here's another miracle," says the rabbi. "My car is destroyed but this bottle of wine didn't break. Surely God wants us to drink the wine to help celebrate our good fortune," he says, handing the bottle to the priest.

The priest nods in agreement, opens the wine, drinks half of it, and hands it back to the rabbi. The rabbi takes it and puts the cap back on.

"Aren't you going to have any? asks the priest.

"Not right now," says the rabbi. "I think I'm going to wait until after the police make their report."

The grass is not greener

Just when you believe you've seen everything, something unexpected occurs, leaving you in disbelief. It was the beginning of the shift, and officers were still arriving on their assigned units. I had just entered mine when I heard a loud scraping sound, as if someone was dragging their boot across the pavement.

I turn around and look just in time to watch an officer stumble across the pavement, trip on the curb, and flop down in the grass. Unsure what the hell just happened, I stand there for a minute to watch.

At this point, I fully anticipated that the officer would stand up and bow his head in shame. We've all stubbed our toes on a crack, failed to notice a dip in the ground, glanced in one direction, and ended up falling. This officer did not get back up. He just lay there motionless in the grass.

I thought, oh shit, this poor bastard had a heart attack and died right on the spot. There was no moaning, no groaning, no flailing of limbs—nothing.

A few staff members rushed to check on the officer, but they had to wait for a lieutenant to arrive first. The staff brought down a wheelchair, assisted in loading the officer into it, and then removed him from the compound.

The staff quickly spread the word that the officer smelled strongly of alcohol and appeared to be intoxicated. The next

question that circulated throughout the institution was, "How did he get here if he was so drunk that he couldn't stand?"

Another staff member quickly answered the question by revealing that the drunk officer had occupied three parking spots. The lieutenant went out and took pictures as proof of him driving there.

When it became clear that the drunk officer couldn't work in that condition, they took him to the hospital and then gave him a ride home. Given the multiple alcohol-related issues on his record, most officers would have faced termination. Instead of firing him, the institution gave him the opportunity to retire in lieu of being terminated.

Pizza boy

This narrative combines nepotism, crime, ignorance, and stupidity into a cohesive whole. The story began when the officer secured a job at the Department of Corrections due to the influence of their father, a high-ranking member of the management team. Despite the officer's unacceptable behavior, he always relied on his father's support for safety when he found himself in trouble.

It didn't take long for him to escalate from ignored minor infractions to a crime that warranted his arrest. One night, the officer had consumed a bit too much alcohol, which led to a heated argument between himself and a police officer at a bar. As the argument intensified, the officer lunged at the police officer, striking him in the face.

Well, this incident landed the officer in jail for assault, but daddy's influence saved his son's ass and his job.

Not long after that incident, the officer, who had been drinking, decided to order some pizza. When the pizza arrived, it just so happened to be a young, adorable female who was still a minor. The officer tried everything he could to lure her inside of his house. Luckily, she had the smarts to not go inside.

What happened next is sickening. The officer grabbed her by the arm and tried to drag her inside the house. Fortunately, she fought fiercely, managed to escape, sprinted to her car, and drove as fast as she could back to the restaurant. Upon her arrival she told her supervisor what happened, and the supervisor immediately called the police.

The correctional officer happened to arrive at the restaurant as the police were taking a statement from the delivery girl.

The correctional officer started apologizing and kissing everyone's ass, likely realizing he had made a serious mistake.

The cop asked him how he got there, given his obvious intoxication. He said he drove there. The cop arrested him for DUI and assault. This time, his father was unable to intervene on his behalf.

Quick, hide the cans

Sometimes management surprises you with the craziest ideas. However, what they did this time was truly brilliant. They arrived at the towers and decided to conduct a surprise search. To ensure the search was successful, they locked down the institution, gathered all the tower officers, and then dispatched a search team. They not only searched the towers but also their ceilings.

The ceilings were like those in a business building. The ceiling consisted of a grid of metal L beams, each consisting of 2 x 2 squares. Once they removed those beams, the secret was revealed.

Every tower contained Playboys, Penthouses, and, most importantly, an abundance of empty beer cans.

People may wonder how they got beer cans into the towers. Well, the answer was simple. The tower officers never checked in. They went straight to the towers. Once they arrived at the towers, they called in to inform control that they were on post.

Once up in the tower, it was easy to kick back, relax, and sip on some suds, and not a single soul would know. The tower even included a fridge and a microwave, allowing you to enjoy a hot dinner while sipping an ice-cold beer.

I must confess that I never took part in the practice and was shocked to learn about it. What baffled me was the officers' decision to store the cans in the ceiling, treating them like trophies. If you brought them in, why not take them back out with you when you left? Unless they were putting in extra hours, it would be the most efficient method to dismiss them.

In all honesty, it might have only been one beer per night. But one beer a night could add up to quite a bit, as this was the first time I ever believed the ceiling was searched. Regardless, I'm confident that the institution began conducting more sporadic searches on both the towers and those who were heading to them.

He won't know

There's nothing wrong with going out with friends, having a wonderful time, and just enjoying the camaraderie. The event could be anything from something simple like a backyard BBQ, a golf game, or a night out at the races. Only your imagination can limit the possibilities.

What is not acceptable is when you plan an event, and people think it's acceptable to take advantage of you. That's exactly what happened to me at an event. My so-called friend at the event was buying drinks with my credit card without my knowledge. They never asked for my permission, never offered to reimburse me, and never made an effort to inform me.

It's not the money that bothers me. A few drinks is really nothing. It's the boldness and the conviction that I will never discover the truth that matters. I would have gone through hell and back to help them, and this is how they ultimately treated me. A slap in the face.

When I discovered what happened the following day, I had the option to file a police report, but I chose not to do so. Little did they know, but buying the drinks without me knowing about it is a felony count of grand larceny because it is a card, possibly identity theft, and possession of stolen property. I didn't go that route, though. I'm not a dirtbag like them.

It may seem like a rant, but this story's lesson is to be selective about your friends. At least a dog will bow its head when it's in trouble; the snakes will look you right in the eye and lie.

That's some good shit

In the field of corrections, a well-known saying goes, "I am a paid observer." In this story, the statement couldn't be more inaccurate.

In corrections, sit-up counts verify that inmates are alive and have not been beaten or intentionally injured themselves.

In this case, the inmate acquired his cellmate's medications without the cellmate's knowledge and took all of them—yes, all of them.

I'm not sure what the medication was, but the inmate leaned up against the wall on his bunk and relaxed. The inmate probably didn't know what the medications were either, but being a drug addict, he didn't care; all he wanted was a high, and he believed he could find it with his cellmate's medication.

Well, at first sight it appears as if the medication did its job and put the inmate to sleep or transported him to a foreign world in another galaxy. For all we knew, he was flying through the stars, high as a kite.

What we do know is that the inmate made it through the first count, which is a sit-up count to make sure the inmates are alive. The officer observed the inmate sitting upright and proceeded with the count, without ever verifying whether the inmate was awake, in good health, experiencing a heart attack, or experiencing any other condition.

Five hours later, the inmate had yet to move from that spot. That alone should have alerted the officer to a potential issue, but it didn't. Once again, the inmate sat through this count, and the officer noticed nothing unusual.

The officer attempted to wake the inmate during the next count later that night, but received no response. Upon poking the inmate and observing his stiffness, the officer determined that something was amiss.

The coroner estimated that the inmate passed away between nine and ten in the morning, with no detection until later that night. How in the hell do you explain that one?

I thought I flushed

Before we begin with this story, we must first understand what Suboxone is. Suboxone contains a combination of buprenorphine and naloxone. Buprenorphine is an opioid medication, sometimes called a narcotic. Naloxone inhibits the effects of opioid medication, such as pain relief and feelings of well-being, which can potentially lead to opioid abuse. We use Suboxone to treat narcotic (opiate) addiction, not as a pain medication.

It was early morning, and the day shift officer departed roll call and made his way to the unit. Upon his arrival, he relieved a response staff officer who was giving a break. As that officer departed the unit, the day shift officer entered the bathroom to put away his belongings, he noticed a Suboxone strip floating in the toilet.

Unsure what to do, the officer notified the captain that he had found Suboxone. He suspected that either the previous officer had left it for an inmate or an inmate had already used it.

That officer informed a friend about the find, and word of it quickly spread.

The officer who brought in the Suboxone heard it on the radio and sprinted towards the unit, intercepting the captain as he made his way to the unit.

The officer clarified that they had access to Suboxone due to their pain and simply forgot to flush the toilet. As stated earlier, we know Suboxone is not meant for pain.

The captain expressed his understanding, as he also takes Suboxone for pain.

The officer's husband repeatedly called the officer a rat and ridiculed him for reporting what he found. What should the officer have done? And why is that officer allowed to bring it inside the institution? **You truly can't make this shit up...**

Lawyer up

Not very often does a smoking deal fall into your hands, so when it does, you must take advantage of it.

Due to a foot surgery, I was working in the mailroom when another officer was assigned to the same location. My partner and I in the mailroom were both thinking, "What are you doing here?"

Well, the officer stated that he injured his knee and was put on light duty.

We both knew it was bullshit, but who are we to decide? I assumed he was here for pencil whipping his checks, as we all knew that's what he did.

After about a week, the officer asked us if we were looking to buy any guns, as he was in urgent need of money.

I asked him what he had for sale, and the only thing that interested me was a Para Ordinance, 1911, Black Ops special edition. I asked how much, and he said seven hundred. Being the kind guy that I am, I offered him six hundred.

He initially declined, but by the end of the day, he asked if the payment would be made in cash that day. I said it would, and he accepted.

About another week passed, and then we found out what he was really in the mailroom for. The officer had been abusing children, and he needed the money to hire a lawyer. If I had known the purpose of the money, I would have offered him four hundred dollars.

The officer eventually disappeared from the institution. We can only speculate that once the evidence proved to be true, they arrested and charged him.

You may be wondering why this particular story is included in this section. The story is included in this section because the officer's actions were only possible if he was either intoxicated or under the influence of another drug, as no rational person would commit such a crime.

Miscellaneous stories

Each story in this section could fit into one of the other categories, but since there are so many elements in each, I decided to make a miscellaneous category. Some are funny, some are sad, but the one thing that they all have in common is that they are all true. Once again, I will remind you that names, places, dates, and anything that could identify the innocent, or the guilty has been deleted so each can enjoy the story without repercussions.

J. R. Harris

An old Italian gentleman lived alone in New Jersey. He wanted to plant his annual tomato garden, but it was very difficult work, as the ground was hard. His only son, Vincent, who used to help him, was in prison. The old man wrote a letter to his son and described his predicament:

Dear Vincent,
I am feeling pretty sad because it looks like I won't be able to plant my tomato garden this year. I'm just getting too old to be digging up a garden plot. I know if you were here my troubles would be over. I know you would be happy to dig the plot for me, like in the old days.
Love, Papa

A few days later he received a letter from his son.

Dear Papa,
Don't dig up that garden. That' s where the bodies are buried.
Love, Vinnie

At 4 a.m. The next morning, FBI agents and local police arrived and dug up the entire area without finding any bodies. They apologized to the old man and left. That same day the old man received another letter from his son.

Dear Papa,
Go ahead and plant the tomatoes now. That's the best I could do under the circumstances.
Love you, Vinnie

Federally funded vacation

Who doesn't like a nice long 12 week vacation? Especially when it's funded by the government and cost you nothing. There were a few stipulations to this paid vacation though which everyone knew, but very few abided by. This stipulation was that you had to have kids at home which needed supervision. What started out as a good idea to help those who really needed it, turned into the greatest moral and ethical collapse of all time. It was so bad; words could not describe the anger and frustration of those who got fucked on a daily basis. Those who took advantage of the system fucked their co-workers with such malice many had PTFD (Post Traumatic Fuck Disorder).

The time frame I am speaking of is one that we know well, covid. Because of covid schools were shut down and children had to stay home. Because of this most parents were scrambling on what they were going to do for babysitters. The idea was good to give employees with children the time off to watch their kids, or so it seemed.

Once the system became operational, the system was overwhelmed with officers who suddenly needed the time off. We had officers whose children were older than14 and couldn't stay home alone for 8 hours. I'm sorry but if your kid cannot stay home alone at that age you failed as a parent. We had officers who did not even have their children as they were with the X but still needed the time off. We had staff whose spouses were teachers and obviously not at work, but they needed the time off. The excuses of why they needed those 12 weeks were unbelievable. What's even crazier is that management said nothing.

Do you think those people stayed home... oh fuck no. They took vacations to Hawaii, Vegas, New Orleans, Sea World, Disneyland, and many more. I could continue but why? Believe you get the point.

For those of us who kept our moral values and went to work we got fucked with the golden schlong. Mandatory overtime daily for 16 hours was the norm. For most people it was 4 days a week and usually asked to work overtime on the 5th. Do you think management helped? Yeah right. They unzipped their pants and said suck it. The only thing they did was to notify you were in the bucket and get pissed if they happen to get stuck once a month. This shit went on and on for what seemed like no end in sight. This was also during the time many staff quit because of the mandatory shot which did not help the situation. I find it rather funny how they think it's okay for them to say they have to be home with their kids, while telling me that time with my family doesn't mean shit.

Eventually, it did come to an end and their solution was to award those who got fucked daily a measly 1500 dollars. Fuck that shit. Keep you god damn blood money and give me the 12 weeks off paid.

See quote from Shawn O'Donnell from the union perspective

I have some pretty good stories of that whole fiasco from the union side of things. When people started getting called out for it (after the fact), the excuses were really out there. That program was split funded by the state and feds. Oregon got a load of cash, earmarked for Covid related things, that program being one of them. Gov Brown stain held tight on as much as she could. That program, Along with the 'work from home' program, really hurt the day to day operations of DOC. Going into bargaining during Covid, there was a lot on infighting about working from home. I brought up that statistically, it doesn't work. I got a lot of push back. Well, now I feel somewhat vindicated. The larger the work pool, the more chance you have of having those individuals that will take advantage of anything they can, while screwing over their coworkers.

A guy is sitting at the doctor's office. The doctor walks in and says, "I have some bad news. I'm afraid you're going to have to stop masturbating." "I don't understand, doc," the patient says. "Why?" "Because," the doctor says. "I'm trying to examine you."

Money clip

On certain days, you hope that karma will repay you for all your charitable deeds. On the flip side, though, you wonder if you should say fuck karma and only worry about yourself. In this particular situation, I sincerely hope that I made the right decision.

I had just gotten off work, and I was walking through the parking lot to my car. Near my car, on the ground, I noticed a money clip, thick with 100 dollar bills, as if it contained someone's entire paycheck. I picked it up and looked around for a likely dropper. Having seen no one, I considered my best course of action.

I could have easily hopped in my car and driven away; no one would have been the wiser. By doing that I would have known that I intentionally fucked over one of my co-workers. I would be unable to gaze at them without questioning whether they are the individual who was unable to make their car payment due to a significant financial loss.

Nope, I did the right thing and walked back into the institution and went to the secretary. I handed them the money clip and told them where I found it in the parking lot. The lady thanked me kindly, then stuck the money clip in an envelope.

About a week passed when I received an envelope. Inside the envelope was a note that read, "Thank you very much. I really appreciate it." There was also a 10 spot.

I'm not telling this story to brag or look for kudos. I'm telling this because I do hope that it was returned to them and not just made to look like it was so I would never

> " Success Is Not Just About Making Money. It's About Making a Difference "
>
> **Unknown**

question where the money went. If the money was indeed returned to them and you are reading this, I would like to say, "You're welcome; we all gotta look out for each other."

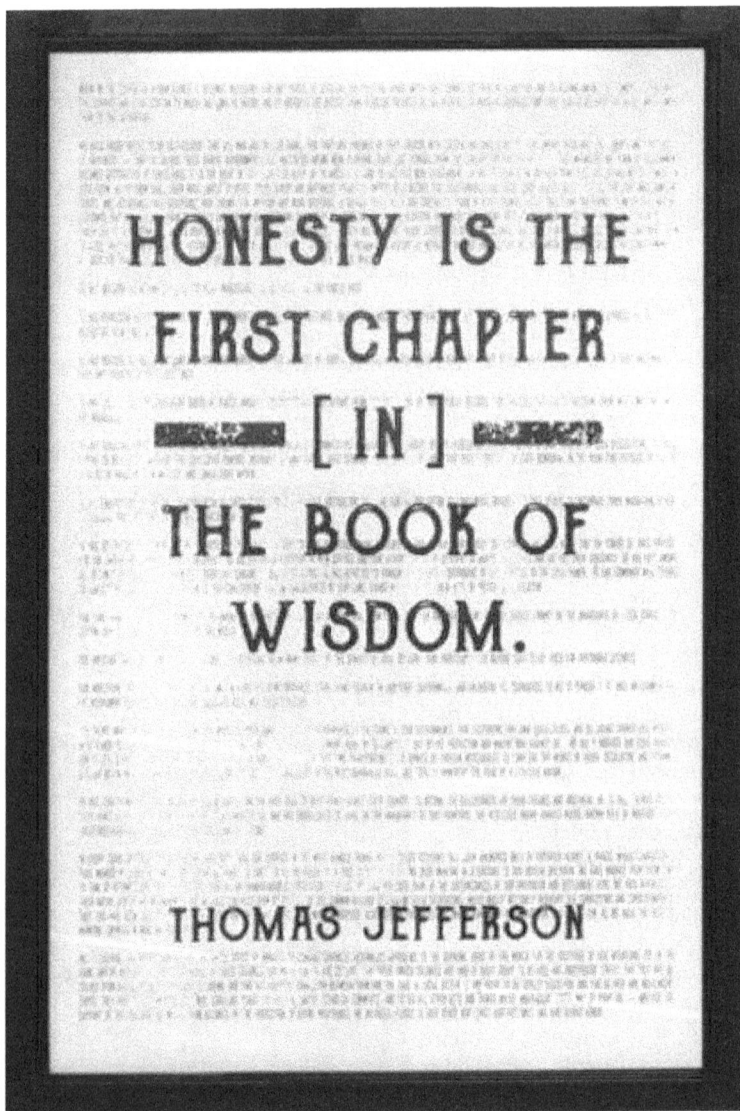

HONESTY IS THE FIRST CHAPTER [IN] THE BOOK OF WISDOM.

THOMAS JEFFERSON

Lost little lamb

Have you ever found yourself in one of those situations where you are stuck with someone who knows absolutely everything, when in fact they don't know a goddamn thing? No matter how many times you try and tell them what is actually occurring, they become defensive and argue with you. This is exactly the position I found myself in one night when I had to do hospital watch with another officer who got mandated.

It all began when we sat down in the vehicle. The officer was already livid, complaining about why we are even going out there because the inmate has already passed on. I said, "No, he didn't." The officer argued, saying the inmate had passed on. I told him that I have been out there every night this week and there is no way he passed on.

When I realized years ago most people are stupid Life got easier

As we were driving out to leave, he asked me to stop at another vehicle, and he asked that officer about the inmate at the hospital and if he had passed away. I said, "No, he has not." The officer actually told me to shut up. I was like, What the fuck? The officer in the other vehicle responds; that's what I heard.

Driving to the hospital, this guy is bitching and moaning about everything under the sun. What I should have done was pull over and say you can drive; hopefully that would shut him up.

We arrive at the hospital, and low and behold, the inmate was awake. I say, "Well, he doesn't look dead to me."

At dinner time, the nurse brings in his food and sits it on the table. The inmate has a hard time eating, so I am trying to help him, and the officer tells me to leave him alone and give him some room.

I said, "Fuck it," and sat down. He can take care of all of this from now on. I don't give a fuck anymore.

Soon, the officer is over there helping him eat. I just chuckled, "I've been here all week; I know what he needs."

We found out shortly after that the inmate was going to be transferred to another hospital. I asked the officer if he wanted to ride in the ambulance or drive the chase vehicle. He decided to ride in the ambulance, as he had never been here before. Fine, give me a break from his ass at least. After the transfer, he calls the lieutenant and asks if I can just drop him off at home. The lieutenant says sure. I should have known right then I was fucked.

We leave the hospital, and not two blocks away he says, "Turn here." My house is a straight shot. I said, "It can't be." He demands that I turn there, then we drive a bit, and he has me turn again, and again, and again. Finally, he says, "I don't know where I'm at."

Well, no shit Sherlock. You already told me you had never been here before, but suddenly, in the dark when you can't see shit and it's raining, it's a straight shot to your house. You really are a special kind of stupid.

I get us going again after wasting a god bit of time on his bullshit, and soon we are back on the highway headed to his house. All in all, that had to be one of the worst nights of my correctional career.

Package size

I was working in the mailroom due to a non-work-related injury. I don't know much about the mailroom other than opening letters, looking for contraband, scanning through the letters, and then putting them back in the envelope.

On this particular day, I was working in the mailroom when the phone rang.

"Officer Harris, mailroom, how can I help you?"

The lady on the other end asked me what is the largest package that she can send in?

Without missing a beat, asking for help, or handing the phone off, I spoke as if I were a mailroom expert. "I don't fucking know."

"Excuse me," the lady said.

I looked at the phone like the lady was stupid, then spoke clearly again. "I said I don't fucking know?"

Another officer who was in the mailroom looked at me with horror in her eyes. Fighting to get out of the chair, she took the phone from me. After a brief discussion about the package's size, everything returned to normal.

Evidently, the lady was dissatisfied with my response and contacted the institution again. Within ten minutes, I received a phone call from the receptionist, informing me that I was no longer permitted to answer the phones.

Score, mission accomplished. I didn't like the damn device anyway.

All about me

Whether we like it or not, you will eventually be required to work overtime in corrections. It happens to everyone; nobody is exempt. You can exert some control over it by volunteering, but even this is not a guarantee.

I put in a significant amount of overtime, so when I received the news that I was the second person stuck, I was a little taken aback, but I accepted the situation. I attend roll call to determine where I'm stuck, and the individual who is stuck first erupts into a hysterical fit of rage, as they believe that they were entitled to be there due to it being their unit.

Ummm, it doesn't work like that. When you are mandated, you go wherever the lieutenant tells you to go.

The lieutenant offered us the option to swap units, which prompted her to humbly and pleadingly ask to be transferred to my unit. I agreed, stating that I don't mind the location; overtime is overtime regardless of its location.

At this point, the unscrupulous, cunning, and dishonest officer resolved to manipulate the system. She reaches out to a fellow officer at her residence, inquiring if they will come in early to get her out as she is mandated.

He said he would, then calls the lieutenant and says he can come in early to get a mandatory out.

The lieutenant thanked him and told him that he would be getting officer Harris out.

The officer called back to his friend, informing her that he would be responsible for my release, not hers.

I received a call from the lieutenant informing me that my relief is on its way.

"Fantastic," I tell myself. "Almost out of here."

She loses her shit because he is not going to get her out. She proceeds to tell him that if he is not going to get her out, then call back and tell the lieutenant that you can't come in for some bullshit reason. If you don't have the balls to do it, then I will call the lieutenant and do it for you."

He calls in and informs the lieutenant that he can't make it due to an unexpected event.

The lieutenant is forced to call me and inform me that the officer is no longer able to make it, and he apologizes for the inconvenience.

This is the moment when the officer truly loses her composure. She calls me up and lets me know that she told the officer to not come in and get me out because she was upset that she was not going to be able to get out.

"What a bitch," I mumble, but there is nothing I can do about it. I even switched posts with her because she wanted to work the unit I was assigned, and this is the way she does me. However, fate ultimately dealt her a harsh blow when I left a few hours later, leaving her to spend the majority of the day on that unit. Had she not told him not to come in, she would have gotten out way sooner. So in the end, she fucked herself.

The jokes never end...

A man purchased a new Mercedes to celebrate his wife leaving him.... He took his new Benz out on the interstate for a nice evening drive. The top was down, the breeze was blowing through what was left of his hair and he decided to open her up. As the needle jumped up to 80 mph, he suddenly saw flashing red and blue lights behind him. *There's no way they can catch a Mercedes*, he thought to himself and opened her up further. The needle hit 90, 100.... Then the reality of the situation hit him. *What am I doing?* he thought and pulled over.

The police cop came up to him, took his license without a word and examined it and the car. "It's been a long hard day, this is the end of my shift and it's Friday. I don't feel like more paperwork, I don't need the frustration or the overtime, so if you can give me a really good excuse for your driving that I haven't heard before, you can go."

The guy thinks about it for a second and says, "Last week my nagging wife ran off with a cop. I was afraid you were trying to give her back!"

"Have a nice weekend," said the officer.

Sheets

Everyone has disagreements. it's how you handle those situations that dictates the outcomes. Some people will admit they're wrong, while others stand their ground believing they're 100% right and refusing to relent their position. It appears the term "we can agree to disagree" got flushed down the proverbial toilet and now floats in a cesspool of piss and shit in a water treatment facility waiting to be cleaned, filtered, and sent out to be used in some other occupation.

So is the case of this incident, which started with a phone call from a friend.

The sun broke the rim of the horizon only minutes earlier when the phone cut loose. Ring… Ring… the phone screamed. Had I known it was my buddy calling and not the lieutenant, I may not have answered the phone. "Officer Harris, How may I help you?"

"Man, you're not going to believe what the fuck happened?" He said.

I knew from the tone of his voice this was going to be good. "Go on."

"I got a call from the Sergeant wanting to finish sheet exchange because they didn't get a chance on swing."

"And?" I asked.

"I jokingly told him it's not my job."

I rubbed my eyes, knowing no good was going to come from this. "What did he say?"

"He ordered me to do it like I'm his bitch. Fuck him, and the sheets."

"Ah shit, here we go," I mumbled.

"The fucker also threatened me," he continued.

"What do you mean, threatened you?" I asked.

"He told me if I didn't do it, he would call the lieutenant and have me written up for insubordination, like we were in the goddamn military or something."

"We are kind of like the military with the chain of command, but really it doesn't mean shit. It's not like you're going to be court marshaled and thrown in the brig," I said with a chuckle.

He laughed, then continued. "I told him fine, call the lieutenant;

"I'll tell him I'm busy doing cell sanitation."

"Well then, there you go," I said.

"That must have pissed him really off because then he threatened to beat my ass."

"What?"

"Yeah," he continued. "He threatened to meet me out in the parking lot when I got off work."

"I don't think he would," I mumbled, watching my orderlies work.

"Regardless, I want you to walk out with me as a witness."

Not really wanting to get involved, I considered my options, which were limited. "Sure, I can do that."

"Thanks," he said.

"Well, I got to go," I said, still trying to compute what I just heard.

As I expected, the sergeant was not in the parking lot, and I never heard any more of it. If I asked, I'm sure the sergeant would have had his own version of what happened. What's sad is it could have been handled differently had he gone and spoke with the officer. Perhaps the officer was having a hell of a morning and was busy as all hell. Too many times have I seen sergeants and above believe they are the all-mighty and what they say is the rule of law.

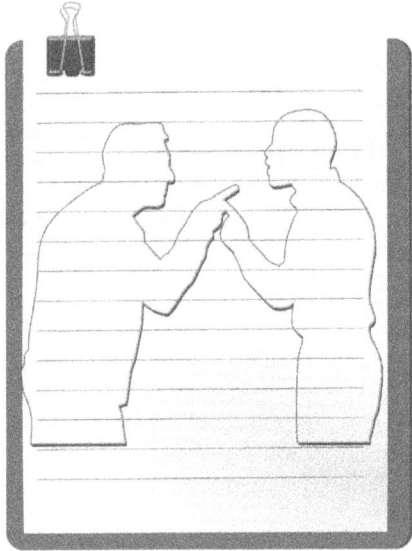

Fuck Harris

There is no shame to admit when it comes to overtime; you always pick the best available spot. This was the case when I entered the roll call rom and was offered overtime in a prime location. Of course I took it. Why wouldn't I? I would have been stupid to let it pass.

At approximately 6:30ish A.M., I received a phone call from the lieutenant informing me that he was going to shut down that post and asked if I wanted another spot. I told him no, and I would be okay. He asked me again, saying that I signed up first so I could have anything that was open. I told him by now anything good had been taking and I didn't want to bump someone, so I would just go home instead.

I thought that was going to be the end of it and planned on going home; that was until about 7:30ish A.M. when the call came over the unit intercom system, "Attention, no WFD today." In the background, you could hear other people talking during the announcement, and then this came over the intercom loud and clear as well. "Fuck Harris, I'm shutting down WFD."

I stood there for a moment, not sure what to say. Did I hear that correctly? I thought. My thoughts were confirmed when an inmate sat up on his bunk and looked at me and said, "Hey Harris, was that about you?"

"Yes, it was," I answered.

Then the phone rang. I answered it. On the other end was another officer laughing while he said, "Fuck Harris."

This was only the first of many phone calls I would receive that morning. With each phone call that came in, the more and more pissed I got.

When I got relieved, I went straight to the superintendent and informed him of what occurred, and I was pissed. He told me that this was completely unacceptable and that he would get to the bottom of it. It appeared to me that he was just as pissed as me, and I honestly thought something might get done.

The next day I was informed that the people in control said that nobody said anything and had no idea what I was talking about. I told him, "If it was never said, then how the fuck did the entire institution hear it?"

He didn't answer and just walked away.

The next day I ran into a sergeant who was working in control that day and told me. "Hey Harris, I just wanted to let you know that it wasn't me that said that."

I told him I knew it wasn't him, and I knew who it was, but it mattered not as nothing was going to happen.

Good ol' high school

On occasion, you open your mouth and insert your foot. Most people attempt to retract their statements, protect their reputation, and remain silent. Oh no, not this incident.

We were enjoying lunch in the staff dining hall when the conversation shifted toward a particular nurse, who was rather large.

I mentioned that I didn't know who she was, as I don't spend much time in medical, so I just sat there quietly and listened.

The officer persisted in his tirade, spreading his arms to illustrate the woman's size and claiming that she qualified for special benefits.

I sat there, baffled by what I was hearing, as I could not recall ever seeing a woman of that size working there.

Another officer was quietly eating at the table, oblivious to the conversation.

The topic of conversation shifted from her size to high school. The officer looked side to side, making sure he had everyone's attention, then spoke, "I attended high school with her. God damn, could she suck a mean dick."

Another officer chimed in, stating that he also attended high school with her and had heard about it, but he never had the opportunity to personally experience it.

The officer who was sitting there quite, put his fork down, and politely said, "That's my mom; I would appreciate you all not talking about her like that."

The officer who was talking about how well she sucked a mean dick never missed a beat as he continued talking about how she could choke it all down.

The officer repeated his request that he refrain from discussing his mother.

I have no idea of the outcome of this, as I got up and left. I wanted no part of this in any way, shape, or form. I could only envision the memos I would need to write.

I'll watch the camera

Working in corrections, there's a certain amount of trust that the public puts in us. The public holds us to a higher standard. The truth is that many correctional officers should live with the people they watch. This is the tale of a sergeant who should consider himself fortunate to hold his position, let alone avoid arrest for such a heinous breach of public trust.

I took on the task of visiting for a single day, as the regular officer had to call in sick. I completed all the usual tasks to prepare for the visit before the operation started. Initially, the operation is typically busy due to the large number of visitors arriving simultaneously, but eventually, the pace slows down. Eventually, you reach a point where your main role is to sit at the desk and watch for any illegal activity.

In the officer's area, the sergeant sits opposite me at the desk. I became bored and decided to chat with him, only to be shocked by what I saw. He had the camera trained on the cleavage of a woman who was quite well-endowed. "What the fuck are you doing?" I asked.

"I'm watching her because I think she has something stuffed down there," he answered.

I called bullshit. "You're watching her because she has the biggest tits in the room."

The sergeant offered me a stern glance.

"If you're that concerned, then get a female officer here and have them do a search," I said.

Right then, he realized he was in trouble.

I went back to my original place, as I wanted no part of this bullshit.

He quickly moved the camera to a different angle, but the tension was still palatable. I didn't care. If he desires to observe tits, there is an abundance of time after work, and there are numerous women who are eager to do so. Work is not the place to indulge in such behavior.

Are you legal

It doesn't matter whether you are a correctional officer, corporal, sergeant, lieutenant, captain, or superintendent. You have zero, none, zilch, or nada authority outside of the institution. I have yet to understand why individuals in positions of authority within the institution suddenly perceive themselves as the local police. For clarification, I have included the differences for your convenience.

Police Officers: Police officers have the authority to make arrests, issue citations, and enforce laws within their designated jurisdiction.

Correctional Officers: Correctional officers do not have the authority to make arrests or enforce laws outside of the correctional facility. Their jurisdiction is limited to the facility and its grounds.

It's imperative that you know the difference so you will understand why this story falls into the category of harassment.

The shift lieutenant repeatedly instructed an officer to ride his motorcycle to work.

The officer was hesitant but eventually gave in to the lieutenant's repeated bantering. On the night he decided to ride it, there was a noticeable shift in the lieutenant's demeanor. No longer did he seem interested in the bike; he seemed more interested in looking at the plate on the motorcycle. NOTE: Some sport bike riders like to keep their plates tucked up underneath the back fender.

Without permission, the lieutenant reached out and pulled down the plate so he could examine it. The lieutenant then regarded the officer as if he were a criminal and informed him that the tag had expired. The owner of the bike might have a temporary permit under the seat, or he might have new tags at home that he simply forgot to put on. No matter, he shouldn't have touched the officer's bike.

I know the lieutenant likes to think he is some form of law enforcement, as when I rode my bike, he wanted to check it out as well. I said, "Sure, let's go."

The plate on my bike is located underneath my storage compartment and is not visible up close. You have to stand back about fifteen feet or so to see it.

The first thing he says isn't, "Damn, that's a good-looking bike.

What year is it? Is it comfortable, or how does it ride?" Those are usually the first questions you ask a bike owner. Nope, not him. The first question he asked was he wanted to know where the plate was.

I told him where to find the plate, but what I should have said was if it was up your ass, you would know where it is. I have nothing to worry about, as I know my plate, license, and tags are all good. This is just another fine example of management abusing their authority in situations that don't concern them..

BIKES ARE LIKE WIVES
IF IT AIN'T YOUR'S DON'T TOUCH

Conclusion

In conclusion, I'd like for you to remember all the dedicated correctional officers who go to work every day to keep those deemed unfit for society locked away safely from the public and to remember that behind all these stories is a face, a name, a person, and a soul who once believed in doing the right things. The purpose of this book is not to hold individuals accountable, but to portray the genuine lives of correctional officers and the challenges we encounter, sometimes from our own colleagues in uniform. With that, I would like to bid a fond farewell and wish you all the best.

Thank You

James R. Harris

He is not crazy, he's a warrior who survived chaos. He is not stupid, he was betrayed by those he trusted most. He is not shy, he is guarding his heart from further harm. He is not angry, he is speaking his truth without apology. He is not stuck in the past, he carries the scars of battles won. He is not delusional, he endured storms most would never survive. He is not weak, his loyalty was his strength. He is not giving up, he's healing, rebuilding, and becoming stronger every day. He is living proof that true strength isn't loud, it's steady, resilient, and unbreakable... he is unstoppable.